the
bean

book

the bean book

over 70 recipes using beans and other pulses

THE LYONS PRESS
Guilford, Connecticut
an imprint of The Globe Pequot Press

First published in Great Britain in 2001
by Hamlyn
a division of Octopus Publishing Group Ltd

The Lyons Press is an imprint of The Globe Pequot Press

Printed in China

ISBN 1-58574-473-5

2 4 6 8 10 9 7 5 3 1

The Library of Congress Cataloguing-in-Publication Data is available on file.

NOTES

1 The American Egg Board advises that eggs should not be consumed raw. This book contains some dishes made with raw or lightly cooked eggs. It is prudent for more vulnerable people such as pregnant and nursing mothers, invalids, the elderly, babies and young children to avoid uncooked or lightly cooked dishes made with eggs.

2 Meat and poultry should be cooked thoroughly. Keep refrigerated until ready for cooking. To test if poultry is cooked, pierce the flesh through the thickest part with a skewer or fork – the juices should run clear, never pink or red.

3 This book includes dishes made with nuts and nut derivatives. It is advisable for those with known allergic reactions to nuts and nut derivatives and those who may be potentially vulnerable to these allergies, such as pregnant and nursing mothers, invalids, the elderly, babies, and children, to avoid dishes made with nuts and nut oils. It is also prudent to check the labels of preprepared ingredients for the possible inclusion of nut derivatives.

Contents

Introduction

The term "bean" is used for both the edible seeds and the seed-bearing pods of various plants (called legumes) belonging to the family Leguminosae. Bean seeds, peas, and lentils are often referred to as pulses.

Bean seeds (usually dried) and bean pods (usually fresh) are readily available. They come in a huge range of shapes, colors, and sizes and are popular worldwide. Each region has its favorite way of using them—falafel and hummus in the Middle East, refried beans in Latin America, dhals in India, bean and pasta soups in Italy, cassoulet in France, pork and bean stews in Eastern Europe. Beans can be served simply, as a side dish, or made into thick soups, stews, and casseroles; they can be puréed or mashed for use in dips and pâtés, or served cold, freshly cooked and marinated, in a substantial salad, a meal in itself.

Brief history

Legumes are among the oldest food crops grown by man. Besides being of nutritional value, they are useful in agriculture for their nitrogen-fixing properties, restoring the soil after use.

The preference for specific beans in various countries today derives largely from the history of their cultivation. Bean varieties have traveled widely since however, and most are now available worldwide.

Fava beans are the oldest-known podded vegetable in Europe and the Middle East, and have been grown and eaten throughout the region since the Bronze Age. The word "bean" on its own originally referred to the fava bean; only when other varieties were introduced from the New World did "fava" become necessary to distinguish it from other species. Despite being a staple food for the poorer masses, the fava bean has had some strange and superstitious beliefs attached to it by various cultures, including an association with death and the supernatural. This may in some part be due to the bean's ability to affect some people with a form of poisoning called favism (*see page 9*).

Varieties of beans belonging to the botanical genus *Phaseolus*, native to Central and South America, were introduced to Europe from the 14th century onward. The haricot bean, first cultivated by the Aztecs, includes a large group of different varieties of green beans and their seeds (*see Haricot bean, page 10*). (The name "haricot" is a French corruption of the Aztec word, *ayacotl*.) These fresh and dried beans overtook the native fava bean in popularity. String beans came later and were initially grown in Europe for their showy flowers rather than as a vegetable.Other legumes with a long history include chickpeas, lentils—their cultivation dates as far back as

6750 B.C. in Iraq—and the soy bean in China—the first written record of which dates back to 2838 B.C. From China, soy bean cultivation spread to Japan and then to Europe in the 17th century. Here, unlike in the East where soy beans are processed into many different products, the dried beans were initially cooked like other beans and quickly disregarded as unpalatable. Western interest in the bean was revived only when its extraordinary nutritive value was scientifically confirmed in the 19th century. Since then scientists and manufacturers have developed a wide variety of soy bean products (*see page 13*).

Nutrition and health

Beans, especially dried ones, are highly nutritious and account for the origin of the expression to be "full of beans", meaning to be lively.

All dried pulses, with the exception of soy beans, have a very similar nutritional content. They are rich in protein, carbohydrates, and dietary fiber, and are low in fat, which is mostly unsaturated. They also supply useful amounts of minerals and vitamins: calcium, iron, phosphorous, magnesium, and some B vitamins. Fresh beans have a different nutritional value because of their high water content. They contain vitamins A and C, but these vitamins decrease once the beans have been picked and are

virtually lost in dried beans. However, many dried pulses—for example adzuki beans, chickpeas, whole lentils, mung, and soy beans—can be sprouted, which makes them rich in both B and C vitamins. Canned and frozen beans retain about half their original vitamin C content.

Dried pulses, except soy beans, contain a higher percentage of protein (about 20 percent) than most other plant foods. However, this protein is "incomplete" or "second class" and needs to be combined with other foods, ideally grains, that complement their various amino acids to produce a "complete" or "first-class" protein with the full complement of amino acids required by the body. The ideal combination of pulses and grains seems to have evolved naturally in meals around the world—for example tortillas and refried beans, dhal and chapatis, and baked beans on toast. In this way, dried beans are an excellent source of protein for vegetarians and those living in regions where protein is scarce or expensive.

Soy beans have a very high protein content (about 35 percent), which is more than other bean proteins, and accounts for its nutritional importance—especially in regions where little meat is eaten. Unlike other beans, the soy bean also has a high fat content (about 20 percent)—used to produce soy bean oil—and is low in carbohydrates.

Nutritional values

Typical nutritional breakdown for dried navy beans (used in canned baked beans) and dried soy beans per 100 g (3½ oz.) dried beans.

	protein	fat	carbohydrate	fiber	iron	calcium
navy beans	22.3 g	1.3 g	50.7 g	24.4 g	6.4 mg	155 mg
soy beans	36.5 g	19.9 g	30.1 g	9.3 g	15.7 mg	277 mg

Source: USDA Nutrient Database

Toxins in beans

Dried beans must be prepared properly as they contain lectin, a toxin that is rendered harmless only during the soaking and cooking processes. In particular, it is not safe to eat raw or undercooked kidney and soy beans.

Red kidney beans contain a toxin in their skins, which can be destroyed by cooking the beans initially at a high temperature, making them completely safe to eat. Canned kidney beans are precooked and safe to use as they are.

Soy beans also require careful cooking. They should be soaked for 8–12 hours, drained and rinsed, then covered with fresh water and brought to the boil. Soy beans should be boiled for the first hour of cooking. They can then be simmered for the remaining 2–3 hours that it takes to cook them. Processed soy products are quite safe to use.

Flatulence

Dried pulses are well known for causing flatulence, thanks to the oligosaccharides they contain. These complex sugars are indigestible by normal stomach enzymes and so pass into the lower intestine where they are fermented by friendly bacteria, resulting in a build-up of gas. Changing the soaking water two or three times improves the digestibility of dried pulses as the sugars that cause flatulence leach into the soaking liquid. The addition of a pinch of aniseed, caraway, cumin, dill, or fennel seeds to the cooking water is also thought to counteract the problem.

Favism

Fava beans are known to provoke a severe allergic reaction called favism in a small group of people of Mediterranean or Middle Eastern origin—the regions where the bean originated. Favism can result in anemia, physical weakness, and jaundice and is thought to be hereditary.

Varieties and Identification

There are two broad categories of beans—those with edible pods (generally available as fresh beans) and those whose seeds only are edible (mostly available as dried beans, but sometimes fresh). Some beans, for example lima beans and fava beans, can be found in both fresh and dried form. Common names of beans can be very confusing, for the same names are often used for different varieties in different countries.

Green bean

This general term covers various fresh beans that have long, edible flat or rounded pods, with small seeds inside. Some beans are skinny, others are much thicker. The pods are usually green although there are purple and pale yellow varieties too. Most green beans are originally from the New World, and many of these are types of haricot bean. The names are used interchangeably: French bean; green bean; runner bean; string bean (originally named for the fibrous indigestible string that ran down the pod's seam, but not generally found now in commercial species); snap bean; and wax bean, a pale yellow variety of green bean. The purple-podded beans look different while raw, but the pods turn green when they are cooked.

Green beans are also readily available frozen or canned. Frozen beans in particular, are a good alternative to fresh.

Lima bean

This bean is named after the capital of Peru, from where cultivation spread slowly northward and to Africa and Asia. There are two distinct varieties—the fordhook and the smaller sieva. Lima beans are popular in the U.S., where they are usually sold shelled and frozen, or fresh in their pods, which should be plump, firm, and dark green. Although young lima beans do not require shelling, they usually are shelled just before cooking to reveal plump, pale green seeds with a slight kidney-shaped curve. Lima beans are also available canned and dried. In the South, dried lima beans are often referred to as butter beans. The large European butter bean, or Madagascar bean, is a close relative to the lima bean and is most often available canned or dried. A traditional way to serve lima beans is combined with corn, molasses, and paprika in the unusual native North American dish, *succotash*.

Fava bean

This flattish bean, also called the broad bean, resembles a very large lima bean and was the original staple of Europe, North Africa, and the Middle East long before the introduction of the haricot bean from the Americas. Fava beans are available fresh, dried, canned, and frozen. The pods of very young fava beans are edible and simply require "topping and tailing"; they can be eaten raw. Old fava beans tend to have a very tough skin, which should be removed by blanching before cooking them.

They can be cooked in a variety of ways; falafel is a well-known Middle Eastern favorite, while in Europe fava beans are traditionally served stewed with ham or bacon and herbs. A small round variety of fava bean is the *ful medame*, used in the Egyptian national dish of the same name, in which the fava beans are baked with eggs and spices.

Butter bean
See Lima bean.

Haricot bean

Originally a native of Central America, the haricot bean (*Phaseolus vulgaris*) includes a large number of varieties—both climbing and bush species—widely grown in the U.S., Europe, and elsewhere. Varieties include certain green beans, kidney, pinto and pink beans, and flageolets (*see individual entries*). Haricot bean seeds (as opposed to the pods) are sold either fresh or after being dried in their pods.

In France and Britain, "haricot bean" generally now refers to small, smooth, white, dried beans, which are oval rather than kidney-shaped. The best of these, the soisson, comes from France and is used in the classic dish, cassoulet.

pinto beans

aduki beans

black-eyed peas

mung beans

red lentils

green lentils

lima beans

flageolet beans

black beans

Varieties and Identification

In the U.S. such haricots are called white beans. Varieties include the navy (or Yankee) bean, used as a staple by the U.S. navy since the mid-1800s, and the pea bean. Both are used to make Boston baked beans and for canning.

Kidney bean

The red kidney bean is a type of haricot bean—firm, with a dark red glossy skin and cream flesh. The smaller, lighter red bean is used in the South for making dishes like red beans and rice. Elsewhere, it is probably best known for its use in chili con carne. It is more readily available dried or canned than fresh.

The black kidney bean, also called the turtle bean, has the same uses as the red kidney bean and the pinto bean and again features in many Latin American dishes, notably the Brazilian national dish *feijoada*.

White kidney, or cannellini, beans are less flavorsome and are available only dried or canned. They are popular in Italian cooking, particularly in salads, casseroles, and soups.

Pinto bean

A variety of haricot bean grown in Latin America and the southwest U.S., this pale pink bean is streaked with reddish-brown. Pinto (Spanish for "painted") beans are widely used in Tex-Mex cooking and Mexican bean dishes, especially *frijoles refritos*, and are often served with rice or used in soups and stews. The pinto bean can be used interchangeably with the pink bean, which is lighter in color before cooking but looks the same afterward. Pinto beans are available in dried form.

Borlotti bean

Another dried bean from the haricot family, this one is very popular in Italy. The bean is light brown or pink and speckled with deeper red. It resembles the pinto bean in appearance, and is typically used in Italian regional stews and soups.

Flageolet bean

Usually white or pale green, this tiny, tender French haricot bean has a creamy, delicate flavor. It is available fresh, dried, canned, and sometimes frozen. It is most often served with lamb or ham.

Cannellini bean

See Kidney bean.

Black-eyed pea

This small whitish/beige bean with a distinctive spot of black at its inner curve is also called the black-eyed bean, cowpea, and, if the "eye" is yellow, yellow-eyed pea. The bean was introduced from Africa to Europe and America via slave traders in the late 17th century. It is generally sold dried although it is available fresh in the South, where it is an essential ingredient in the dish hoppin' John, traditionally served on New Year's Day to bring good luck.

Soy bean (soybean, soy pea, soja, soi)

There are over a thousand varieties of soy beans, ranging in size and color (white, yellow, green, red, brown, and black). The soy bean has a high nutritive value and is used to produce a wide variety of products including tofu (soy bean curd), soy bean oil, soy flour, soy milk (useful for those allergic to dairy products), textured vegetable protein (TVP), fermented black beans and bean pastes, and sauces such as soy sauce, shoyu, miso, kecap, and tamari. Soy beans can be soaked and cooked like any other dried beans for use in soups, stews, and casseroles, although they are quite tough. They can also be sprouted to produce bean sprouts, and used in salads or as a cooked vegetable. Fresh soy beans are not generally available except in Asian or speciality produce markets.

Salted black bean

This is a small soy bean, which is fermented and salted. Salted black beans have a strong flavor and are used in Chinese cooking as a savory seasoning. They are available dried and canned.

Adzuki bean (asuki bean, aduki bean)

This small, dried, dark red starchy bean is particularly popular in Japanese and Chinese cooking and can be purchased whole or powdered in Asian food stores. The bean's sweet flavor has led to its use in oriental confectionery, and its flour is used for making cakes and pastries.

Mung bean

A small cylindrical bean, most commonly olive-green in color with a yellow interior, but brown and black varieties exist. Widely used in Asian cooking, whole mung beans are a popular ingredient in soups, stews, and pilafs. They are often used in Europe to produce bean sprouts.

Chickpea

Although not actually a bean, this small round, irregularly shaped, pale brown legume with its firm texture and mild, nutty flavor, is used in similar ways. Chickpeas (also called garbanzo beans, ceci, and, in India, chana) are used extensively in Mediterranean countries, India, and the Middle East—in salads, soups, and stews and in dishes such as hummus. Chickpeas can be ground to produce gram flour, or besan, which is used extensively in Indian cooking. Chickpeas are available canned and dried; dried chickpeas need lengthy soaking and simmering to become really tender and perfectly delicious.

Varieties and Identification

Lentils

Available both whole and split, dried lentils are popular in parts of Europe and are a staple throughout much of the Middle East and India. They require no soaking and disintegrate quite quickly on cooking. They can be used as a side dish (puréed or whole and combined with vegetables), in salads, soups, and stews. Lentils are used in Indian cookery to make various spicy dhals ("dhal" in India is the general term for split pulses, as well as the dish made from them). The most familiar varieties of lentil include the small reddish-orange split lentil, originally from India; the large, flat, green-brown Continental lentil; and the very tiny, grey-green Puy lentil from France.

Baked beans

The canned baked beans in tomato sauce so familiar today are produced from U.S.-grown navy and pea beans, which are varieties of haricot bean. The product's origins lie in a traditional New England dish called Boston baked beans. The original recipe involved baking navy beans or the smaller pea beans with salt pork, mustard, spices, molasses, and brown sugar in a slow oven for hours until tender. It was traditionally made by Puritan Bostonian women to be eaten on Saturday night; the leftovers were served with heavy Boston brown bread on the Sabbath when cooking was forbidden. Canned baked beans are available with

reduced or no added salt and sugar, and with extra ingredients such as pork sausages or bacon; organic baked beans are available, too. Like all beans, canned baked beans have good nutritive values. A ¾-cup serving of baked beans provides nearly half of the recommended daily fiber intake and more protein than an egg or a cup of milk.

Choosing and storing

Fresh beans start to convert their sugar into starch from the moment they are picked. This process alters their taste and texture, so the fresher they are the better. Freshly picked peas or fava beans are infintely sweeter, crisper, and more tender than those bought at the supermarket. Freezing halts the sugar-to-starch process so frozen beans are a good alternative to fresh.

Fresh beans

When buying any fresh beans, select ones that are crisp, brightly colored, and free of blemishes. A fresh green bean will snap rather than bend if it is fresh. Green beans can be stored in the refrigerator, in an airtight container or tightly wrapped in a plastic bag for up to 5 days. After this, their color and flavor begin to diminish.

Avoid fresh fava beans whose pods are bulging with beans—this indicates age, and mature beans are woolly and tasteless. Fresh fava beans can be kept

in the refrigerator for 3–4 days; lima bean pods can be refrigerated in a plastic bag for up to a week.

Dried pulses

Shop for dried pulses where you know the turnover is brisk. Most varieties are available in supermarkets but those found in "ethnic" stores or delicatessens selling their best national products, will probably be of better quality. Dried beans should be plump and brightly colored with a soft sheen to their skin. Avoid any that are wrinkled, chipped, or cracked, as these are probably quite old.

Dried pulses have a long shelf life and will keep well for up to a year if kept in a dry, airtight container at room temperature and away from the light. However, it is best to eat them as fresh as possible since they do toughen with age and older ones will take longer to cook.

Preparing and Cooking

To prepare fresh green beans, cut off their tips (known as "top and tail"), and remove any strings—a string will come away if you pull downward as you remove the top or tail. Cut the beans thinly either diagonally across the pod or lengthwise. Gently simmer, steam, microwave or stir-fry briefly until slightly crisp to the bite—take care not to overcook them. If the beans are to be served cold in a salad, plunging them into cold water immediately after cooking will help them retain their color.

Cook lima beans briefly in boiling salted water. Similarly, young fava beans can be cooked in their pods in boiling salted water for 10–12 minutes until tender. Mature fava beans need to be shelled then cooked for about 5 minutes. Drain the cooked mature beans then rinse under cold running water. Remove their whitish, rather tough outer skins to reveal the bright green, velvety bean inside.

Soaking dried pulses

Dried pulses are available prepackaged or in bulk. Many need to be soaked in water for several hours or overnight to rehydrate before cooking. Follow the package or recipe instructions for best results. Dried beans labeled "quick-cooking" have been presoaked and redried before packaging; they require no presoaking and so take less time to prepare. However, they are not as firm as ordinary dried beans.

In the past, dried pulses had to be picked over before use to extract small pieces of grit, tiny sticks, and ungerminated seeds. This is rarely necessary nowadays. However, put them in a sieve and rinse thoroughly to remove any surface dust or dirt. Lentils, green and yellow split peas, black-eyed beans, and mung beans are ready to be cooked once rinsed; other dried pulses require soaking first. Soaking times can be 4–12 hours, depending on the type and age of the pulse—soy beans and chickpeas are the hardest pulses and need the longest soaking. During the soaking process remove any immature or overdry specimens that won't cook properly, which float to the surface, and change the water two or three times to help counteract flatulence (*see page 9*).

There are two soaking methods: the conventional one involves putting the pulses in a large bowl, covering them with four times their volume of cold water and leaving them to stand. It is often convenient to soak pulses overnight—the longer they are allowed to soak, the softer they become and the quicker they cook. The alternative, quick-soak method involves putting the pulses in a saucepan with four times their volume of cold, unsalted water. Bring to a boil, then boil vigorously for 5 minutes. Cover the pan, remove from the heat, and allow the pulses to stand for about 1 hour.

Soaked pulses are ready to cook when they are plump and fully swollen, with smooth skins. Dried pulses will roughly double in bulk during soaking. Left to soak in hot conditions, dried pulses may start to ferment and the soaking water will appear frothy. If this happens put the bowl in the refrigerator.

Bean safety

Boil soaked red kidney beans vigorously for 10 minutes at the start of cooking to destroy the toxins on their skins.

Cooking dried beans and chickpeas

Once the pulses have been soaked, drain—always discard the soaking water—and rinse in fresh water. Place in a saucepan and cover with more fresh water until the water level is about 1–2 inches above the pulses. This is sufficient to prevent the pulses from drying out; too much water allows more protein and carbohydrates to leach out of them, thus diminishing their nutritional value.

Bring the pulses to a boil then reduce the heat and simmer gently. The exception to this is red kidney beans, which must be boiled vigorously for 10 minutes before simmering to ensure that any toxins on the outside skins of the beans are completely destroyed. At one

Preparing and Cooking

time this 10-minute vigorous boiling was the accepted practice for all beans but it is now not considered necessary, although some cooks still advise it for aduki, black kidney, and borlotti beans.

Continue simmering the beans gently until soft, frequently removing the scum that forms on the surface. Adding a little oil to the cooking liquid can help prevent the scum from forming. The beans are cooked when soft to the bite and evenly colored all the way through. The length of cooking time varies according to the type of pulse, the quantity of pulses being cooked, and their age—old pulses can take twice as long to cook.

Seasonings such as garlic, onion, oregano, parsley, or thyme can be added during cooking, but not acidic ingredients, such as tomatoes, vinegar, wine or lemon juice, which will increase the cooking time. It is better to add these ingredients only when the beans are almost tender. Similarly, while salt is necessary to bring out the flavor of dried beans, it can slow down the cooking and is best added toward the end when you can better gauge how much is required. At one time a pinch of bicarbonate of soda was added to speed up cooking. This is no longer recommended as it destroys nutrients. Take care not to overcook dried pulses since, with the exception of chickpeas, they will disintegrate and become mushy.

Cooked dried beans absorb other flavors well—even more so if the flavoring is added while the cooked beans are still hot. If the beans need to be cold, leave to cool in their cooking liquid to keep them from drying out and their skins splitting.

Cooking lentils

To cook whole lentils, simply bring them to a boil in plenty of water (or stock or wine) and cook until just soft. To cook split lentils for a purée or pâté, measure the water exactly according to the recipe, or the end result may be too sloppy.

Canned pulses

Canned pulses are already cooked and are a quick and convenient alternative to dried. Simply drain and rinse well to remove the canning liquid. To substitute canned beans for dried, remember that the weight of dried beans roughly doubles during soaking and cooking so a recipe that calls for 1 cup dried beans would require about 2 cups drained, canned beans. Check the labels of canned pulses for additives—many varieties have added salt or sugar.

Keeping cooked beans

Cooked dried beans keep well so it is worth cooking a large batch in one go and storing the excess in usable quantities. Plain boiled beans can be drained and stored in an airtight plastic container in the refrigerator for 5–6 days, beans cooked with onion will keep half that time. Alternatively, freeze cooked beans, either in their cooking liquid or drained, in airtight plastic containers for up to 6 months. Allow them to thaw overnight in the refrigerator, or for 2–3 hours at room temperature, or defrost them in a microwave. When reheating cooked beans, add 2–3 tablespoons of water.

Cooked bean dishes also keep well and can be kept refrigerated for 4–5 days.

Organic beans

Food that is certified and labeled "organic" has been produced by strictly defined methods. Thus, organic beans have been grown without the use of artificial chemical fertilizers and pesticides, and they are free from any genetically modified organisms (GMOs). Organic processed foods such as canned baked beans contain no artificial flavorings or colorings.

Various types of organic beans are now available—in canned, dried, and frozen form—for example canned cut green beans, lima beans, lentils, baked beans, and chickpeas, and dried soy, black-eyed, butter, haricot, kidney, and pinto beans. It is likely that many more bean varieties will become increasingly available in organic form.

Basic Recipes

Makes approx. 1 cup / Preparation time: 3 minutes

Harissa

Harissa is a fiery red paste, a blend of red chilies, garlic, and spices, widely used in North African cooking. It is used during the preparation of dishes and appears in small bowls on the table as a condiment. It is available commercially or you can make your own.

2 red bell peppers, roasted and skinned

2 tablespoons fresh red chilies, chopped, seeds
   retained

1–2 garlic cloves, crushed

½ teaspoon coriander seeds, toasted

2 teaspoons caraway seeds

olive oil

salt

1. Place the red peppers, the chilies and their seeds, garlic, coriander and caraway seeds, and a pinch of salt in a blender or food processor. Blend the ingredients together, adding enough olive oil to make a thick paste.
2. Spoon the harissa into a small, clean, dry jar and pour a layer of olive oil over the top to seal. Cover with a tight-fitting lid and store in the refrigerator.

Makes 10 lemons / Preparation time: 10 minutes

Preserved Lemons

10 lemons

coarse salt

1. Put 2 teaspoons coarse salt into a sterilized Mason jar. Holding one lemon over a plate to catch the juice, cut it lengthwise as if about to quarter it, but do not cut all the way through—leave the pieces joined. Ease out any seeds. Pack 2 tablespoons salt into the cuts, then close them and place the lemon in the jar.
2. Repeat with the remaining lemons, packing them in tightly, and pressing each layer down hard before adding the next layer, until the jar is full. Squeeze another lemon and pour the juice over the fruit. Sprinkle with more coarse salt and fill up with boiling water to cover the lemons. Close the jar tightly and keep in a warmish place for 3-4 weeks. Do not worry if, on longer storage, a lacy white film appears on top of the jar or on the lemons; it is quite harmless. Simply rinse it off.

Makes 4⅓ cups / Preparation time: 5—10 minutes / Cooking time: about 45 minutes

Vegetable Stock

1 lb chopped mixed vegetables, such as equal
  quantities of carrots, leeks, celery, onion, and
  mushrooms
1 garlic clove
6 peppercorns
1 bouquet garni (2 parsley sprigs, 2 thyme sprigs
  and 1 bay leaf)
5 cups water

1. Place the chopped vegetables and garlic in a large saucepan and add the peppercorns and bouquet garni.
2. Cover with the water. Bring to a boil and simmer gently for 30 minutes, skimming off any scum when necessary. Strain and cool the stock completely before refrigerating.

Makes approx 1 cup / Preparation time: 5–10 minutes

Pesto

50 g (2 oz) basil leaves
1 garlic clove, crushed
2 tablespoons pine nuts
¼ teaspoon sea salt
6–8 tablespoons extra virgin olive oil
2 tablespoons freshly grated Parmesan cheese
pepper

1. Grind the basil, garlic, pine nuts, and sea salt in a mortar or food processor to form a fairly smooth paste. Slowly add the oil until you reach the required texture, soft but not runny, and then add the cheese and pepper to taste. Transfer to a bowl and cover the surface with plastic wrap.
2. Serve tossed with freshly cooked pasta, spooned onto soups, or with grilled fish or chicken. Pesto can be kept chilled for up to 3 days in the refrigerator.

VARIATION
To make red pesto, add 25 g (1 oz) drained and chopped sun-dried tomatoes in oil to the basil and continue as above, omitting the Parmesan.

Soups
and
Appetizers

Serves: 8 very generously / Preparation time: 20 minutes, plus overnight soaking / Cooking time: about 3 hours

La Ribollita

This very filling bean and cabbage soup is one of Tuscany's most famous soups. La ribollita means "reboiled" and refers to the fact that, traditionally, the soup was reheated and served day after day. To make it stretch further when there was little meat and vegetables to spare, bread was added. Even now, the soup is made the day before it is needed then reheated. It is ladled over toasted garlic bread, drizzled with olive oil, and served with plenty of Parmesan. Strictly speaking, the soup should be made with the delicious black Tuscan cabbage called cavolo nero, but Savoy cabbage is a good substitute.

⅓ cup extra virgin olive oil

1 onion, finely chopped

1 carrot, chopped

1 celery stalk, chopped

2 leeks, trimmed, cleaned, and finely chopped

4 garlic cloves, finely chopped

1 small white cabbage, shredded

1 large potato, chopped

4 zucchini, chopped

2 cups dried cannellini beans, soaked overnight,
    drained, and rinsed

1¾ cups strained tomatoes

2 sprigs of rosemary

2 sprigs of thyme

2 sprigs of sage

1 dried red chili

8¾ cups water

4 cups cavolo nero or Savoy cabbage, finely
    shredded

salt and pepper

To serve:

⅓ cup extra virgin olive oil, plus extra for
    drizzling

8 thick slices of crusty white country-style bread

1 garlic clove, bruised

freshly grated Parmesan cheese

1. Heat the oil in a heavy-based saucepan. Add the onion, carrot, and celery and cook gently for about 10 minutes, stirring frequently. Next add the leeks and garlic and cook for another 10 minutes. Add the white cabbage, potato, and zucchini, stir well and cook for a further 10 minutes, stirring frequently.

2. Stir in the beans, tomatoes, rosemary, thyme, sage, dried red chili, salt, and plenty of pepper. Cover with the water (the vegetables should be well covered) and bring to the boil, then reduce the heat and simmer, covered, for at least 2 hours, until the beans are very soft.

3. Remove 2–3 ladlefuls of soup, mash it well or purée in a blender or food processor then return to the soup. Stir in the cavolo nero or Savoy cabbage and simmer for another 15 minutes. Leave the soup to cool then refrigerate overnight.

4. The next day, slowly reheat the soup and stir in the olive oil. Toast the slices of bread and rub them with the bruised garlic. Arrange the bread in the base of a tureen or in individual bowls and ladle the soup over it. Drizzle with olive oil and serve with plenty of freshly grated Parmesan.

Lima Bean and Sun-dried Tomato Soup

Although it takes only a few minutes to prepare, this chunky soup distinctly resembles a robust Italian minestrone. It also makes a worthy main course served with bread and plenty of Parmesan.

⅓ cup extra virgin olive oil

1 onion, finely chopped

2 celery stalks, thinly sliced

2 garlic cloves, thinly sliced

2 x 15-ounce cans lima beans, drained and rinsed

½ cup sun-dried tomato purée

3¾ cups Vegetable Stock (see page 21)

2 tablespoons chopped rosemary or thyme

salt and pepper

Parmesan cheese shavings, to serve

1. Heat the oil in a saucepan. Add the onion and sauté for 3 minutes until softened. Add the celery and garlic and sauté for 2 minutes.

2. Add the lima beans, sun-dried tomato purée, vegetable stock, rosemary or thyme, and a little salt and pepper. Bring to the boil, then reduce the heat, cover and simmer gently for 15 minutes. Serve sprinkled with Parmesan shavings.

Minestrone Soup

**Minestrone actually improves in flavor when it is made in advance and reheated.
Cover and store in the refrigerator so that the flavors can blend.**

¼ cup extra virgin olive oil

1 onion, diced

1 garlic clove, crushed

2 celery stalks, chopped

1 leek, trimmed, cleaned, and finely sliced

1 carrot, chopped

1 x 14.5-ounce can chopped tomatoes

2½ cups chicken or Vegetable Stock
   (see page 21)

1 zucchini, diced

½ small cabbage, shredded

1 bay leaf

¾ cup canned navy beans, drained and rinsed

¾ cup dried spaghetti, broken into small pieces

2 tablespoons chopped flat leaf parsley

salt and pepper

To serve:
¼ cup Parmesan cheese, freshly grated

bruschetta

1. Heat the oil in a saucepan. Add the onion, garlic, celery, leek, and carrot and sauté for 3 minutes.
2. Add the canned tomatoes, stock, zucchini, cabbage, bay leaf, and navy beans. Bring to the boil and simmer for 10 minutes.
3. Add the broken spaghetti and season with salt and pepper to taste. Stir well and cook for a further 8 minutes. Keep stirring, as the soup may stick to the bottom of the pan.
4. Just before serving, add the chopped parsley and stir well. Serve with grated Parmesan and bruschetta.

FOOD FACT

Bruschetta comprises thick slices of country-style bread, toasted, rubbed with cut garlic, and brushed with a well-flavored olive oil. Italian breads such as focaccia or ciabatta or French *pain de campagne* or a baguette are suitable alternatives to serve with this chunky soup.

White Bean Soup with Garlic Sauce

More or less identical soups based on dried white beans are popular in Italy, particularly Tuscany, as well as in Greece and Turkey.

¾ cup extra virgin olive oil

2 garlic cloves, crushed

1 bay leaf

leaves from 2 sprigs of thyme and 2 sprigs
    of oregano

1 sage leaf, chopped

3 cups dried cannellini beans or borlotti beans,
    soaked overnight, drained, and rinsed

7½ cups boiling water

1 large onion, chopped

2 carrots, chopped

1 stalk of celery, chopped

salt and pepper

finely chopped parsley, to garnish

Garlic sauce:

3 large egg yolks

½ cup lemon juice

3 garlic cloves, crushed

¾ cup unsalted butter, melted until just bubbling

salt and pepper

1. Heat 4 tablespoons of the oil in a large heavy-based saucepan. Add the garlic, herbs, and beans and cook, stirring frequently, for about 5 minutes. Add the boiling water and simmer until the beans are tender—about 1 hour, depending on their age; add a little more water during cooking if necessary. Discard the bay leaf.

2. Meanwhile, heat the remaining oil in a frying pan, add the onion, carrots, and celery, cover tightly and cook over a low heat, stirring occasionally, until soft—about 20 minutes.

3. Stir the vegetables into the beans and purée half the mixture in a blender or food processor. Return the purée to the remaining bean mixture in the pan, season, and reheat gently.

4. To make the garlic sauce, mix the egg yolks, lemon juice, garlic, and seasoning in a blender or food processor. With the motor running, slowly add the melted butter and continue mixing for a few minutes to make a thick, creamy sauce. Transfer to a warm bowl.

5. To serve, pour the soup into warm bowls. Add a spoonful of the sauce to each and sprinkle with finely chopped parsley.

Serves 6 / Preparation time: 20 minutes / Cooking time: 45 minutes

Mexican Soup with Avocado Salsa

A fiery soup that reflects the rich and contrasting flavors of
Latin America, cooled by the subtle smoothness of an avocado salsa.

¼ cup sunflower oil

1 large onion, chopped

2 garlic cloves, crushed

2 teaspoons ground coriander

1 teaspoon ground cumin

1 red bell pepper, cored, seeded, and diced

3 red chilies, seeded and sliced

1 x 15-ounce can red kidney beans, drained
   and rinsed

3 cups tomato juice

2–4 tablespoons hot sauce

¼ cup tortilla chips, crushed

salt and pepper

cilantro sprigs, to garnish

Avocado salsa:

1 small ripe avocado

4 scallions, finely chopped

2 tablespoons lemon juice

2 tablespoons chopped fresh cilantro

salt and pepper

1. Heat the oil in a large, heavy-based saucepan. Add the onion, garlic, spices, red pepper, and two-thirds of the chilies, and fry gently for 10 minutes. Add the kidney beans, tomato juice, and hot sauce. Bring to a boil, cover, and simmer gently for 30 minutes.

2. Meanwhile, make the avocado salsa. Peel, pit and finely dice the avocado. Place in a bowl and combine it with the scallions, lemon juice, and fresh cilantro. Season with salt and pepper to taste, cover the bowl with plastic wrap, and set aside.

3. Purée the soup in a blender or food processor, together with the crushed tortilla chips. Return the soup to a clean saucepan, season to taste, and heat through. Serve the soup at once with the avocado salsa, garnished with the reserved chili slices and some sprigs of cilantro.

Serves 4 / Preparation time: 15 minutes, plus overnight soaking / Cooking time: 2¼ hours

Tasty Bean Soup

3 cups dried navy beans, soaked overnight,
   drained, and rinsed
8¾ cups water
1 carrot, chopped
1 onion, quartered
1 bouquet garni
1 cup cooked smoked ham, cubed
3 tablespoons butter
2 shallots, finely chopped
1 garlic clove, crushed
2 tablespoons chopped parsley, plus extra
   to garnish
olive oil, for drizzling
salt and pepper
croûtons, to serve

1. Place the beans in a large saucepan with the water and bring to the boil over a medium heat. Boil for 1½ hours, or until the beans are just tender.
2. Add the carrot, onion, bouquet garni, and cubed ham and simmer for 20–30 minutes. Discard the bouquet garni, then pour the soup into a blender or food processor. Purée until smooth, working in batches if necessary. Return the purée to the pan and reheat over a medium heat.
3. Meanwhile, melt the butter in a heavy-based pan and gently fry the chopped shallots and garlic until golden but not browned. Add the chopped parsley and mix together quickly. Add half the shallot mixture to the bean purée.
4. Mix well with a wooden spoon, season with salt and pepper, then pour into warm bowls. Sprinkle with croûtons, spooning the remaining shallot mixture onto them. Serve the soup hot, drizzled with olive oil and garnished with parsley.

Serves 6 / Preparation time: 15 minutes / Cooking time: about 50 minutes

Curried Green Bean Soup

¼ cup butter or margarine

1 garlic clove, crushed

1 onion, chopped

2 tablespoons mild curry powder

3¾ cups Vegetable Stock
  (see page 21)

1 teaspoon chopped fresh marjoram or
  ½ teaspoon dried marjoram

1 bay leaf

1 pound round green or French beans, trimmed
  and cut into 1½-inch pieces

2–2½ cups potatoes, peeled
  and cubed

salt

⅔ cup sour cream, to garnish

1. Melt the butter or margarine in a large saucepan and cook the garlic and onion over a moderate heat, until soft but not browned. Stir in the curry powder and cook for a further 2 minutes.

2. Pour in the vegetable stock. Add the marjoram, bay leaf, beans, and potatoes, with salt to taste. Bring the mixture to a boil, then reduce the heat, cover the pan, and simmer for 45 minutes, or until the vegetables are soft. Remove the bay leaf.

3. Purée the mixture in a blender or food processor, working in batches if necessary. Return the puréed soup to the pan. Stir well and heat gently, without boiling. Serve the soup in warm bowls, each garnished with a swirl of sour cream.

Serves 4 / Preparation time: 10 minutes / Cooking time: 15 minutes

Black Bean Soup with Soba Noodles

½ pound dried soba noodles

2 tablespoons peanut or vegetable oil

1 bunch of scallions, sliced

2 garlic cloves, roughly chopped

1 red chili, seeded and sliced

1½ inch piece of fresh ginger, peeled and grated

½ cup black bean sauce or black bean stir-fry sauce

3 cups Vegetable Stock (see page 21)

1½ cups bok choy or spring greens, shredded

2 teaspoons soy sauce

1 teaspoon superfine sugar

¼ cup raw, unsalted shelled peanuts

1. Cook the noodles in a saucepan of boiling water for about 5 minutes, or until just tender.
2. Meanwhile, heat the oil in a saucepan. Add the scallions and garlic and sauté gently for 1 minute.
3. Add the red chili, fresh ginger, black bean sauce, and vegetable stock and bring to a boil. Stir in the bok choy or spring greens, soy sauce, superfine sugar, and peanuts; reduce the heat and simmer gently, uncovered, for 4 minutes.
4. Drain the noodles and pile into serving bowls. Ladle the soup over the noodles and serve immediately.

FOOD FACT

Soba noodles, traditional in Japanese cooking, are made from buckwheat and whole-wheat flour, giving them a nutty flavor without the dryness of many wholemeal pastas.

Serves 4 / Preparation time: 3 minutes

Garlic, Herb, and Bean Pâté

If you have only a few minutes to put together a snack or appetizer, this recipe is an ideal solution. Serve with some slices of warm bread or crisp breads.

1 x 15-ounce can flageolet or navy beans,
   drained and rinsed
½ cup cream cheese
2 garlic cloves, chopped
⅓ cup **Pesto (see page 21)**
2 scallions, chopped
salt and pepper
chopped flat leaf parsley, to garnish (optional)

To serve:
½ cup arugula leaves
16 radishes
8 crisp breads

1. Place the beans, cream cheese, garlic, and pesto in a blender or food processor and process until combined.
2. Add the scallions and season with salt and pepper and process for 10 seconds. Turn into a serving dish and chill until ready to serve. Serve with the arugula leaves and crisp breads, scattered with chopped parsley, if desired.

Bessara

2 cups dried fava beans, soaked overnight,
   drained, and rinsed
3 garlic cloves, crushed
1 teaspoon cumin seeds
extra virgin olive oil, for mixing and drizzling
salt

To serve:
za'atar (wild thyme) or mixed dried thyme,
   marjoram, and oregano
warm bread
mixture of ground cumin, cayenne pepper,
   and salt

This fava bean dip is as popular in North Africa
as hummus is in the Middle East. The taste is
similar, too. In Morocco, the dip is served with
warm bread, which is first dipped into a mixture
of ground spices before scooping up the purée.

1. Place the dried fava beans, garlic, and cumin seeds in a saucepan. Add enough
   cold water to just cover and bring to the boil. Cover the saucepan and simmer for
   1–2 hours—depending on the age and quality of the beans—until tender.
2. Drain the bean mixture, reserving the liquid. Rub the beans through a sieve, or
   purée them in a blender or food processor, adding enough of the reserved bean
   liquid and olive oil to make a cream. Season with salt to taste.
3. Serve the dip warm with extra oil trickled over the top and sprinkled with *za'atar* or
   a mixture of dried thyme, marjoram, and oregano. Accompany with warm bread
   and a small bowl of mixed ground cumin, cayenne pepper, and salt.

Serves 4–6 / Preparation time: 10 minutes, plus overnight soaking / Cooking time: 2½ hours

Refried Beans

This is a very popular dish in the Southwest and in Mexico, where it is known as *frijoles refritos.* The recipe involves frying beans that have been boiled and mashed.

2 cups dried pinto beans, soaked overnight, drained and rinsed
4 garlic cloves, crushed
1 bay leaf
4 tablespoons lard or bacon fat
1½ cups onion, chopped
salt and pepper

To garnish:
sour cream
cilantro sprigs
crushed mixed peppercorns

1. Place the beans in a large saucepan with the garlic and bay leaf. Cover with cold water and bring to the boil. Boil briskly for 10 minutes, then reduce the heat to a bare simmer and cook gently for about 2 hours, until the beans are very tender.
2. Drain the beans, reserving the cooking liquid. Discard the bay leaf. Mash the beans coarsely with a potato masher, or process in a blender or food processor, adding some of the reserved cooking liquid if necessary until the desired consistency is achieved.
3. Melt the lard or bacon fat in a frying pan. Add the onion and sauté, stirring, until soft. Add the mashed beans and seasoning and mix well. Simmer until piping hot, continue to mash and add more liquid as necessary.
4. Serve the beans hot, topped with sour cream, garnished with cilantro sprigs and crushed mixed peppercorns.

Serves 4–6 / Preparation time: 10 minutes / Cooking time: 10 minutes

Chorizo with Fava Beans

Tapas bars serve this dish, or different versions of it, all over Spain. (See also page 41.)

2 cups shelled young fava beans

2 tablespoons extra virgin olive oil

2 garlic cloves, roughly chopped

4 ounces spicy chorizo, cut into slices about
   ¼-inch thick

2 tablespoons chopped dill

2 tablespoons chopped mint

¼ cup lemon juice

salt and pepper

crusty bread, to serve

1. Blanch the fava beans in a saucepan of lightly salted boiling water for 1 minute. Drain, rinse immediately under cold running water, and drain again. Dry well.

2. Heat the oil in a frying pan, add the garlic, and fry gently for 2–3 minutes until softened, then discard. Increase the heat, add the sliced chorizo, and stir-fry for 2–3 minutes, until it is golden and has released some of its oil.

3. Stir in the blanched beans and cook for a further 2–3 minutes, then add the herbs and lemon juice and season to taste with salt and pepper. Mix well. Serve warm with crusty bread.

FOOD FACT

Chorizo is a cured or smoked Spanish salami-style sausage, made with coarsely chopped pork and flavored with paprika, black pepper, and garlic. Chorizo can be eaten raw or used as an ingredient in cooking.

Serves 4 / Preparation time: 15 minutes / Cooking time: 10 minutes

Nut Koftas with Minted Yogurt

5–6 tablespoons peanut oil or vegetable oil

1 onion, chopped

½ teaspoon dried chili flakes

2 garlic cloves, roughly chopped

2 tablespoons medium curry paste

1 x 15-ounce can borlotti beans or cannellini
   beans, drained and rinsed

1 cup ground almonds

¾ cup chopped honey-roast or salted almonds

1 small egg

¾ cup Greek or plain yogurt

¼ cup chopped mint

2 tablespoons lemon juice

salt and pepper

warm naan bread, to serve

sprigs of mint, to garnish

1. Soak 8 bamboo skewers in hot water while preparing the koftas. Alternatively, use metal skewers, which do not require presoaking. Heat 3 tablespoons of the oil in a frying pan, add the onion and sauté for 4 minutes. Add the dried chili flakes, garlic, and curry paste and sauté for 1 minute.

2. Transfer to a blender or food processor with the beans, ground almonds, chopped almonds, egg, and a little salt and pepper and process until the mixture starts to bind together.

3. Using lightly floured hands, take about one-eighth of the mixture and mold it around a skewer, forming it into a sausage shape about 1 inch thick. Make 7 more koftas in the same way.

4. Place on a foil-lined baking pan and brush with 1 tablespoon of the remaining oil. Cook under a preheated broiler for about 5 minutes, until golden, turning once.

5. Meanwhile, mix together the yogurt and mint in a small serving bowl and season to taste with salt and pepper. In a separate bowl, mix together the remaining oil, the lemon juice and a little salt and pepper.

6. Brush the koftas with the lemon dressing and serve on warm naan bread, garnished with sprigs of mint. Serve the yogurt dressing separately.

Fava Beans with Ham

Around the Mediterranean region there are innumerable variations on the theme of fava beans and ham or bacon. Some are more or less just the beans and ham; others have extra ingredients such as breadcrumbs and chopped hard-boiled egg, or carrots and potatoes. This Spanish version is colorful and tasty.

¼ cup extra virgin olive oil

4 large scallions, finely chopped

1 red bell pepper, cored, seeded, and diced

2 ounces serrano ham, diced

4 cups shelled fava beans

about ¾ cup medium-bodied dry
   white wine

salt and pepper

1. Heat the oil in a saucepan. Add the scallions, red pepper, and ham and cook for 3 minutes.
2. Stir in the beans for 1 minute, then add enough wine to cover the vegetables. Bring quickly to a boil, cover the pan, and simmer gently until the beans are tender, about 15–20 minutes. Uncover and boil off any excess liquid, if necessary. Add pepper and salt if necessary—this will depend on the saltiness of the ham. Cool slightly before serving.

VARIATION

Greek Fava Beans with Dill: Gently cook 2 bunches of sliced, plump scallions in ⅓ cup extra virgin olive oil in a heavy-based pan, until soft. Stir in 5 cups shelled fresh young broad beans and cook gently for 2–3 minutes. Add ¼–⅓ cup chopped dill, salt and pepper, and enough water to just cover the beans. Cover and cook gently until the beans are tender. Serve with Greek ewes' milk yogurt.

Brown Beans and Egg with Lemon and Parsley Dressing

This dish makes a great starter or side salad. Health food stores and delicatessens are the most likely to stock brown beans. The canned variety tend to be large, flattish and quite bland, hence this spiced, tangy dressing. Canned red kidney beans or lima beans make a good substitute for brown beans.

1 x 15-ounce can brown beans, drained and
   rinsed
1 small pickle, roughly chopped
2 hard-boiled eggs, roughly chopped
salt and pepper
wholegrain bread, to serve

Dressing:
4 garlic cloves, crushed
1 teaspoon cumin seeds
½ bunch of scallions, thinly sliced
small handful of parsley, chopped
2 tablespoons lemon juice
2 teaspoons Harissa (see page 20)
½ cup extra virgin olive oil

1. To make the dressing, in a large bowl mix together the garlic, cumin seeds, scallions, parsley, lemon juice, harissa and oil.
2. Mix the beans, pickle, and eggs together in another bowl, and season to taste with salt and pepper. Toss together gently, transfer to the bowl of dressing and mix thoroughly. Serve with wholegrain bread.

2

Vegetarian Entrées

Black Beans and Rice Cooked in Stout

1 teaspoon cumin seeds

1 teaspoon coriander seeds

⅓ cup extra virgin olive oil

2 onions, chopped

3 garlic cloves, crushed

1 green chili, seeded and finely chopped

½ teaspoon chili powder

2 teaspoons thyme leaves

1 pound dried black kidney beans, soaked
    overnight, drained, and rinsed

2 bay leaves

¼ cup molasses

1 lb tomatoes, peeled and chopped

1¼ cups stout or Guinness

4⅓ cups water

¾ cup long grain rice

½ cup chopped cilantro

salt and pepper

Salsa:

4 scallions, finely sliced

1 garlic clove, chopped

4 tomatoes, chopped

1 tablespoon chopped cilantro

⅓ cup canned corn kernels, drained

2 tablespoons fresh lime juice

1. Place the cumin and coriander seeds in a frying pan and dry-fry over a moderate heat, stirring, for 1–2 minutes until fragrant—do not let them burn. Leave to cool, then grind to a powder in a spice grinder or using a pestle and mortar. Alternatively, put them in a small bowl and crush them with the end of a rolling pin. Set aside.

2. Heat the oil in a large flameproof casserole. Add the onions, garlic, green chili, chili powder, and thyme and cook for 6–8 minutes until softened. Add the beans, the ground cumin and coriander seeds, and the remaining ingredients, except the rice and cilantro.

3. Bring to a boil, then reduce the heat, cover, and simmer over a very low heat for 1½–2 hours. Check occasionally and top up with boiling water if the mixture seems dry.

4. Add the rice and season with salt and pepper to taste. Cover and cook for a further 30 minutes, or until the beans and rice are very tender. Remove from the heat and stir in the chopped cilantro. Cover and leave for 5 minutes.

5. To prepare the salsa, mix all the ingredients together in a bowl. Serve the salsa as an accompaniment to the beans and rice.

Zucchini and Bean Provençal

1½ cups dried cannellini beans, soaked
   overnight, drained and rinsed

⅓ cup extra virgin olive oil

2 onions, sliced

2 garlic cloves, chopped

1 pound zucchini, diced

1 x 14.5-ounce can chopped tomatoes

¼ cup tomato purée

2 teaspoons chopped oregano or thyme

1 bouquet garni

½ cup black olives, halved and pitted

salt and pepper

sprigs of oregano and oregano leaves, to garnish

1. Place the beans in a large saucepan, cover with fresh water and bring to a boil. Cover and simmer for ¾–1 hour until almost tender, adding salt toward the end of the cooking time. Drain, reserving ⅔ cup of the cooking liquid.

2. Meanwhile, heat the oil in a saucepan and fry the onions until soft but not browned. Add the garlic and zucchini and fry gently, stirring occasionally, for a further 15 minutes.

3. Add the tomatoes, tomato purée, oregano or thyme, bouquet garni, salt and pepper, the drained beans, and reserved liquid. Cover and simmer for 20 minutes, adding the olives 5 minutes before the end of the cooking time. Serve immediately, garnished with oregano sprigs and leaves.

Braised Soy Beans with Shiitake Mushrooms and Spinach

This delightful combination of ingredients and flavors provides a tasty and nutritious dish. It is easy to prepare and makes an ideal mid-week supper dish.

1½ cups soy beans, soaked overnight, drained, and rinsed

⅓ cup extra virgin olive oil

1 garlic clove, chopped

1 teaspoon grated fresh ginger

2 red chilies, seeded and chopped

1 cup shiitake mushrooms, sliced

4 ripe tomatoes, skinned, seeded, and chopped

¼ cup dark soy sauce

¼ cup dry sherry

2 cups spinach leaves, washed and shredded

1. Place the beans in a saucepan with plenty of cold water. Bring to a boil and boil rapidly for 10 minutes, then reduce the heat, cover, and simmer for 1 hour, or until the beans are tender. Drain, reserving ⅔ cup of the cooking liquid.
2. Heat the oil in a large frying pan. Add the garlic, ginger, and chilies and fry for 3 minutes. Add the mushrooms and fry for a further 5 minutes until tender.
3. Add the tomatoes, beans, reserved liquid, soy sauce, and sherry and bring to a boil. Cover and simmer for 15 minutes.
4. Stir in the spinach and heat through for 2–3 minutes until the spinach has wilted. Serve at once.

Serves 4 as a supper dish, 4–6 as a side dish / Preparation time: 10 minutes / Cooking time: 10 minutes

Mixed Bean Ratatouille

Served with a generous topping of freshly grated Parmesan and with crusty French bread, this dish makes a nutritious vegetarian supper. Ring the changes with the ingredients if you like, using different kinds of canned beans, or substituting another fresh vegetable such as snow peas or baby corn for the green beans.

1½ cups green beans, trimmed and halved

¼ cup vegetable oil

1 onion, finely chopped

2 garlic cloves, crushed

1 x 14.5-ounce can tomatoes

¼ cup tomato purée

1 teaspoon dried mixed herbs

¼–½ teaspoon sugar, according to taste

1 x 15-ounce can cannellini beans, drained and rinsed

¼ cup chopped basil, plus extra to garnish

salt and pepper

1. Blanch the halved green beans in a saucepan of lightly salted boiling water for 2 minutes. Drain, rinse immediately under cold running water, and drain again. Set aside.
2. Heat the oil in a saucepan. Add the onion and garlic and fry for 2–3 minutes, or until softened, but not browned.
3. Add the tomatoes, stir to mix with the onion and garlic, and break them up with a wooden spoon. Add the tomato purée, dried mixed herbs, sugar, and salt and pepper to taste. Bring to a boil, stirring constantly.
4. Add the green beans and canned beans to the saucepan. Toss until piping hot and coated in the tomato sauce. Remove from the heat and stir in the basil. Taste for seasoning and adjust if necessary. Serve at once, garnished with basil.

**Serves 8 / Preparation time: 15 minutes, plus overnight soaking /
Cooking time: 2¾ hours / Oven temperature: 300°F**

Bean Tagine

Tagine is the traditional name for both a North African cooking pot and the thick
stew of meat and/or vegetables cooked slowly within it. An authentic everyday
tagine is a shallow round earthenware pot with a tall conical lid.

1 pound dried red or white kidney beans, soaked
  overnight, drained, and rinsed

2 celery stalks, halved

2 bay leaves

4 sprigs of parsley

½ cup extra virgin olive oil

1 pound onions, chopped

5 garlic cloves, crushed

2 red chilies, seeded and chopped

4 red bell peppers, cored, seeded, and chopped

1 tablespoon paprika

large handful of mixed chopped mint, parsley,
  and cilantro

salt and pepper

mint leaves, to garnish

Harissa (see page 20), to serve

Tomato sauce:

1 x 28-ounce can chopped tomatoes

¼ cup extra virgin olive oil

4 sprigs of parsley

2 tablespoons sugar

1. Boil the beans vigorously in a large saucepan of unsalted water for 10 minutes
   then drain. Tie the celery, bay leaves, and parsley together with kitchen string.
   Cover the beans with fresh unsalted water, add the celery and herbs, and simmer
   for about 1 hour until the beans are just tender. Drain, reserving the cooking
   liquid, and discard the celery and herbs.

2. Meanwhile, make the sauce. Empty the tomatoes and their juice into a saucepan,
   add the oil, parsley, and sugar and bring to a boil then simmer, uncovered, for
   about 20 minutes until thick.

3. Heat the oil in a heavy-based flameproof casserole. Add the onions, garlic, chilies,
   red bell peppers, and paprika and cook gently for 5 minutes. Stir in the beans, the
   tomato sauce, and enough of the reserved cooking liquid to just cover the beans.
   Season with salt and pepper, cover, and cook in a preheated oven at 300°F for
   1½ hours, stirring occasionally.

4. Just before serving, stir in the mint, parsley, and cilantro. Garnish with the mint
   leaves and serve with a bowl of harissa.

Serves 4 / Preparation time: 15 minutes, plus overnight soaking / Cooking time: about 1¼ hours

2 cups dried lima or flageolet beans, soaked
    overnight, drained, and rinsed

⅓ cup butter

3 garlic cloves, crushed

2 shallots or 1 small onion, finely chopped

2 small fennel bulbs, finely sliced

1 red bell pepper, cored, seeded, and chopped

3 fresh ears of corn, husk and silk removed, cut
    into 1-inch rounds, or ¾ cup canned or frozen
    corn kernels, defrosted if frozen

3¼ cups Vegetable Stock (see page 21)

¼ cup sherry or white wine vinegar

salt and pepper

Fennel and Corn Succotash

Succotash is a traditional native American vegetable stew. The key ingredients are lima beans and corn, although other beans—haricot, flageolet, black beans, black-eyed peas, or a mixture of two or three varieties—can also be used. This version includes the aniseed flavor of fennel bulbs, which goes particularly well with the corn.

1. Place the beans in a large saucepan with sufficient water to cover. Bring to a boil, reduce the heat, cover the pan, and simmer for ¾–1 hour, or until tender. Drain and set aside.

2. Meanwhile, melt the butter in a large, heavy-based saucepan. Add the garlic and shallots or onion and cook for 5 minutes until lightly browned. Add the fennel and red bell pepper and cook for 15–20 minutes until softened.

3. Add the corn, if using fresh, and the vegetable stock; season to taste. Bring to a boil, reduce the heat, cover, and simmer for 20–30 minutes until the corn is tender. Remove the lid, add the drained beans, the canned or defrosted frozen corn, if using, and the vinegar.

4. Bring the succotash back to a boil and cook for about 5 minutes until the liquid has reduced and thickened slightly. Adjust the seasoning to taste and serve hot.

Serves 6 / Preparation time: 15 minutes / Cooking time: about 50 minutes

Breton Beans with Cheese and Herb Crust

⅓ cup extra virgin olive oil

2 large onions, finely sliced

2–3 garlic cloves, chopped

2 large zucchini, cut into ½-inch dice

2 red bell peppers, cored, seeded, and diced

1 x 28-ounce can chopped tomatoes

2 tablespoons tomato purée

2 x 15-ounce cans lima or other white beans,
    drained and rinsed

⅔ cup Vegetable Stock (see page 21)

2 tablespoons finely chopped parsley

2 bay leaves

1 teaspoon sugar

salt and pepper

mixed salad leaves, to serve (optional)

Cheese and herb crust:

1 small baguette, very thinly sliced

¼ cup extra virgin olive oil

¼ cup finely chopped basil

2 tablespoons finely chopped parsley

¼ cup Parmesan cheese, finely grated

1. Heat the oil in a large saucepan or flameproof casserole dish and fry the onions and garlic until soft but not browned. Add the zucchini and continue to fry for a few minutes until it begins to brown. Add all the remaining ingredients except salt and stir well to combine.

2. Bring to the boil, reduce the heat, cover and simmer until the tomatoes are thick and pulpy and the flavors blended—about 30–40 minutes. Taste and adjust the seasoning, adding salt if necessary.

3. Uncover the stew. To make the cheese and herb crust, brush the bread slices with oil, arrange on top of the stew and scatter with the herbs and Parmesan. Place the pan under a preheated broiler and toast until the bread is golden brown and crisp. Serve immediately with mixed salad leaves, if desired.

Serves 4 / Preparation time: 10 minutes / Cooking time: 50–55 minutes

Orzo Pilaf with Beans and Mint

This is a slightly unusual pilaf using orzo, a tiny rice-shaped pasta, sometimes called risi, and lots of fresh mint. Orzo is available from Italian delicatessens.

½ cup extra virgin olive oil

1 onion, finely chopped

2 leeks, trimmed, cleaned, and sliced

2 garlic cloves, crushed

½ teaspoon ground cumin

pinch of saffron threads

¾ pound orzo

2 sprigs of mint, plus ½ cup
   chopped mint

1¼ cups Vegetable Stock (see page 21)

2 cups green beans, trimmed

½ cup pine nuts, toasted and chopped

2 tablespoons butter

salt and pepper

1. Heat the oil in a large frying pan and fry the onion, leeks, garlic, cumin, and saffron for 10 minutes, until the vegetables are softened but not browned.

2. Add the orzo and stir-fry for 1 minute, until all the grains are glossy. Add the sprigs of mint and vegetable stock and bring to the boil. Cover and simmer for 15–20 minutes, until the orzo is cooked and most of the liquid has been absorbed.

3. Meanwhile, blanch the beans in a saucepan of lightly salted boiling water for 3–4 minutes until al dente. Drain well.

4. Stir the beans into the orzo with the pine nuts, chopped mint, and butter, and season with salt and pepper. Cover and cook over a very low heat for 10 minutes. Remove from the heat but leave to stand for a further 10 minutes before serving.

**Serves 6–8 / Preparation time: 15 minutes /
Cooking time: 2 hours / Oven temperature: 350°F**

Speedy Mixed Baked Beans

1 x 15-ounce can red kidney beans

1 x 15-ounce can navy beans

1 x 15-ounce can adzuki beans or mung beans

1 cup strained tomatoes

¼ cup molasses

1 tablespoon wholegrain mustard

2 tablespoons vegetarian Worcestershire sauce
   or dark soy sauce

½ teaspoon salt

pinch of ground cloves

1 large onion, finely chopped

2 carrots, diced

2 celery stalks, chopped

2 bay leaves

½ cup chopped parsley

To serve:

grated vegetarian Cheddar cheese, (optional)

crusty bread

You may look at the cooking time and decide "speedy" is a slight exaggeration, but the traditional method for Boston baked beans (the precursor of today's canned baked beans in tomato sauce) takes 6 hours to cook, plus overnight soaking of the beans.

1. Strain the liquid from the canned beans and pour half into a bowl, discarding the rest. Whisk the strained tomatoes, molasses, mustard, Worcestershire or soy sauce, salt, and cloves into the liquid until evenly combined.
2. Place the beans and all the remaining ingredients except the parsley into a casserole and stir in the liquid. Cover with a tight-fitting lid.
3. Transfer to a preheated oven, 350°F, and bake for 2 hours. Stir in the chopped parsley and serve in warm bowls topped with the cheese, if using, and accompanied by crusty bread.

VARIATION

Crusted Beans: Combine ½ cup fresh whole-wheat breadcrumbs with ½ cup grated vegetarian Cheddar and 2 tablespoons ground almonds. Sprinkle over the beans after 1½ hours and return to the oven, uncovered, for a further 30 minutes to crisp up the topping.

Penne with Fava Beans and Artichoke Pesto

¾ pound dried penne

3 cups frozen fava beans

¾ cup marinated charred artichokes, roughly chopped

1 garlic clove, chopped

1 tablespoon parsley, chopped

2 tablespoons pine nuts

1 tablespoon pecorino cheese, grated, plus extra to serve

⅔ cup extra virgin olive oil

salt and pepper

1. Cook the pasta in a large saucepan of lightly salted boiling water for 10–12 minutes, or according to package instructions, until tender but still firm to the bite. At the same time, blanch the fava beans in a saucepan of lightly salted boiling water for 3 minutes. Drain and set aside.

2. Meanwhile, put the artichokes, garlic, parsley, and pine nuts in a blender or food processor and process until fairly smooth. Transfer the mixture to a bowl and stir in the pecorino and oil and season to taste with salt and pepper.

3. Drain the pasta, reserving ½ cup of the cooking liquid, and return it to the pan. Add the artichoke pesto mixture, the fava beans, and the reserved cooking liquid and season to taste with pepper. Toss over a medium heat until warmed through. Serve with extra grated pecorino.

FOOD FACT

Marinated charred artichokes are often sold in jars. If you cannot find them, use canned artichoke hearts instead.

**Serves 4 / Preparation time: 10 minutes, plus overnight soaking /
Cooking time: 3¼–3¾ hours / Oven temperature: 300°F**

Lima Beans in Tomato Sauce

2 cups dried lima beans, soaked overnight,
   drained, and rinsed
⅓ cup extra virgin olive oil, plus extra
   to serve
1 small onion, finely chopped
2 garlic cloves, crushed
¼ teaspoon dried chili flakes
1 x 7-ounce can chopped tomatoes
2 tablespoons tomato purée
2 tablespoons dried oregano, plus extra to serve
salt and pepper

1. Place the beans in a large saucepan and cover generously with cold water. Bring to a boil then simmer for 1¼–1½ hours, until they start to feel tender.
2. Drain the beans, reserving the cooking liquid. Place the beans in a casserole with the oil, onion, garlic, dried chili flakes, tomatoes, tomato purée, and oregano and season with salt and pepper.
3. Add enough of the reserved cooking liquid to cover the beans, then bake, covered, in a preheated oven at 300°F for 1½ hours. Remove the lid and cook for a further 30–45 minutes, until the liquid is reduced and thickened. Serve the beans drizzled with a little olive oil and sprinkled with some more dried oregano.

Cannellini Beans with Leeks and Arugula

The creaminess of the beans and their sauce is nicely balanced by the peppery
arugula, stirred in at the last minute until it has just wilted.

1 cup dried cannellini beans, soaked overnight,
   drained, and rinsed

5 cups water

¼ cup walnut oil

2 leeks, trimmed, cleaned, and sliced

2 tablespoons mustard seeds

1 garlic clove, crushed

1 cup green beans, trimmed and halved

⅓ cup heavy cream

2 cups arugula

¼ cup snipped chives

salt and pepper

1. Place the beans in a saucepan with the water. Bring to a boil and boil rapidly for 10 minutes. Reduce the heat and simmer gently for 45–50 minutes until the beans are tender.

2. Strain the liquid from the beans into a pan and boil it rapidly until reduced to 1¼ cups. Reserve.

3. Heat the oil in a saucepan and fry the leeks, mustard seeds, and garlic for 5 minutes. Add the drained beans, green beans, and reduced stock and simmer gently for 5 minutes until the green beans are tender. Remove from the heat. Strain the liquid into a small saucepan, add the cream, and boil for 2–3 minutes until slightly reduced.

4. Stir the arugula and chives into the beans and drizzle the sauce over them. Season to taste and serve at once.

Fava Bean, Lemon, and Parmesan Risotto

2 tablespoons butter

¼ cup extra virgin olive oil

1 onion, chopped

2 garlic cloves, crushed

1⅔ cups risotto rice

⅔ cup dry white wine

5 cups hot Vegetable Stock
   (see page 21)

1⅓ cups fresh or frozen fava beans

¼ cup Parmesan cheese, grated, plus extra
   to serve

finely grated zest and juice of 1 lemon

salt and pepper

thyme leaves, to garnish

FOOD FACT

Risotto rice absorbs a large quantity of liquid during cooking. The grains of rice swell; they remain separate yet stick together to make a creamy risotto in which the rice is soft but firm, not sticky or mushy. Arborio, Vialone Nano, and Carnaroli are the three Italian varieties suitable for risotto making.

1. Melt the butter with the oil in a large, heavy-based saucepan. Add the onion and garlic and sauté gently for 3 minutes. Add the rice and cook for 1 minute, stirring.

2. Add the wine and cook, stirring, until the wine has been absorbed. Add a little stock and cook, stirring, until almost absorbed. Continue in the same way, gradually adding more stock, until half the stock is used. Stir in the beans.

3. Gradually add the remaining stock, a little at a time, until the mixture is thickened and creamy but still retaining a little bite. This will take 15–18 minutes. Stir in the Parmesan, lemon zest, and juice, and season to taste with salt and pepper. Turn out onto warm serving plates, sprinkle with thyme, and serve with extra Parmesan.

Black Bean and Cabbage Stew

½ cup extra virgin olive oil

1 large onion, chopped

1 leek, trimmed, cleaned, and chopped

3 garlic cloves, sliced

2 tablespoons paprika

¼ cup chopped marjoram or thyme

1¼ pounds potatoes, cut into small chunks

1 x 15-ounce can black beans or black-eyed
   peas, drained and rinsed

4½ cups Vegetable Stock (see page 21)

3 cups cabbage or spring greens, shredded

salt and pepper

crusty bread, to serve

1. Heat the oil in a large saucepan. Add the onion and leek and sauté gently for 3 minutes. Add the garlic and paprika and sauté for 2 minutes.

2. Add the marjoram or thyme, potatoes, beans, and vegetable stock and bring to the boil. Reduce the heat, cover, and simmer gently for about 10 minutes until the potatoes have softened.

3. Add the cabbage or spring greens and season to taste with salt and pepper. Simmer for 5 minutes longer and serve with crusty bread.

Serves 4 / Preparation time: 10 minutes / Cooking time: 22 minutes

Red Beans with Coconut and Cashews

⅓ cup peanut or vegetable oil

2 onions, chopped

2 small carrots, thinly sliced

3 garlic cloves, crushed

1 red bell pepper, cored, seeded, and chopped

2 bay leaves

2 tablespoons paprika

⅓ cup tomato purée

1 x 14-fl. oz. can coconut milk

1 x 7-ounce can chopped tomatoes

⅔ cup Vegetable Stock (see page 21)

1 x 15-ounce can red kidney beans, drained and rinsed

1 cup unsalted, shelled cashews, toasted

small handful of cilantro, roughly chopped

salt and pepper

boiled black or white rice, to serve

1. Heat the oil in a large saucepan. Add the onions and carrots and sauté for 3 minutes. Add the garlic, red bell pepper, and bay leaves and sauté for 5 minutes, or until the vegetables are soft and well browned.

2. Stir in the paprika, tomato purée, coconut milk, tomatoes, vegetable stock, and beans and bring to a boil. Reduce the heat and simmer, uncovered, for 12 minutes, or until the vegetables are tender.

3. Stir in the cashews and cilantro, season to taste with salt and pepper and heat through for 2 minutes. Serve with boiled rice.

Serves 2–3 / Preparation time: 5 minutes / Cooking time: 30 minutes

Cannellini Beans on Toast

This is another delicious quick and easy version of Boston baked beans, on which the commercial variety is based. Slightly spicy and sweet, it is comfort food at its best.

¼ cup peanut or vegetable oil

1 onion, chopped

1 celery stalk, thinly sliced

1 teaspoon cornstarch

¼ cup water

1 x 15-ounce can cannellini beans, drained
  and rinsed

1 x 7-ounce can chopped tomatoes

1¼ cups Vegetable Stock (see page 21)

2 tablespoons coarse grain mustard

2 tablespoons molasses

2 tablespoons tomato ketchup

2 tablespoons vegetarian Worcestershire sauce

salt and pepper

toasted chunky bread, to serve

1. Heat the oil in a saucepan. Add the onion and celery and sauté for 5 minutes until golden. Blend the cornstarch with the water and add to the pan with all the remaining ingredients.
2. Bring to the boil, reduce the heat slightly, and cook, uncovered, for about 20 minutes, stirring frequently, until the mixture is thickened and pulpy. Pile on toast to serve.

Serves 4 / Preparation time: 15 minutes / Cooking time: 15 minutes

Red Pepper and Bean Cakes with Lemon Mayonnaise

Pack these crisp bean cakes into warm pita bread and serve with salad for a fairly substantial lunch or supper dish. Any unbaked bean cakes will keep in the refrigerator, covered with parchment paper, for a day or so.

¾ cup green beans, trimmed and roughly chopped

¼ cup peanut or vegetable oil

1 red bell pepper, cored, seeded, and diced

4 garlic cloves, crushed

2 teaspoons mild chili powder

1 x 15-ounce can red kidney beans, drained and rinsed

¾ cup fresh white breadcrumbs

1 egg yolk

oil, for shallow-frying

salt and pepper

Lemon mayonnaise:

½ cup mayonnaise

finely grated zest of 1 lemon

1 teaspoon lemon juice

salt and pepper

1. Blanch the green beans in a saucepan of lightly salted boiling water for 1–2 minutes until softened. Drain.
2. Meanwhile, heat the oil in a frying pan and sauté the bell pepper, garlic, and chili powder for 2 minutes.
3. Transfer the mixture to a blender or food processor and add the red kidney beans, breadcrumbs, and egg yolk. Process very briefly until the ingredients are coarsely chopped. Add the drained beans, season to taste with salt and pepper and process until the ingredients are just combined.
4. Turn the mixture into a bowl and divide into 8 portions. Using lightly floured hands, shape the portions into little cakes.
5. Mix the mayonnaise with the lemon zest and juice, and season to taste with salt and pepper.
6. Heat the oil for frying in a large frying pan and pan-fry the cakes for about 3 minutes on each side until crisp and golden. Serve with the lemon mayonnaise.

Serves 4 / Preparation time: 10 minutes / Cooking time: 25 minutes

Bean and Beer Casserole with Baby Dumplings

½ cup peanut or vegetable oil

1 onion, sliced

1 celery stalk, sliced

1 parsnip, sliced

1 x 15-ounce can mixed beans, drained
and rinsed

1 x 15-ounce can baked beans in tomato sauce

1 cup Guinness or stout

1 cup Vegetable Stock (see page 21)

½ cup roughly chopped herbs (such as rosemary,
marjoram, thyme)

1½ cups self-rising flour

⅓ cup vegetable shortening

¼ cup coarse grain mustard

1 cup cold water

salt and pepper

1. Heat the oil in a large saucepan or flameproof casserole. Add the onion, celery, and parsnip and sauté for 3 minutes. Add the mixed beans, baked beans, beer, vegetable stock, and ⅓ cup of the herbs. Bring to a boil and let the mixture bubble, uncovered, for 8–10 minutes, or until slightly thickened.

2. Meanwhile, mix the flour, shortening, mustard, remaining herbs, and a little salt and pepper in a bowl with enough of the cold water to make a soft dough.

3. Evenly distribute 8 spoonfuls of the dough in the saucepan or casserole and cover with a lid. Cook for 10 minutes more, or until the dumplings are light and fluffy. Serve immediately.

Black Bean Chili

2 cups dried black kidney beans, soaked
  overnight, drained, and rinsed

6¼ cups water

½ cup extra virgin olive oil

2 cups small mushrooms, halved

1 large onion, chopped

2 garlic cloves, crushed

2 large potatoes, cubed

1 red or green bell pepper, cored, seeded,
  and diced

2 teaspoons ground coriander

1 teaspoon ground cumin

2 teaspoons hot chili powder

2 cups strained tomatoes

2 tablespoons fresh lime juice

2 tablespoons bittersweet chocolate, chopped

¼ cup chopped cilantro

Avocado salsa:

1 small ripe avocado

4 scallions, chopped finely

2 tablespoons lemon juice

2 tablespoons chopped cilantro

salt and pepper

1. Place the beans in a saucepan with the water. Bring to a boil then boil rapidly for 10 minutes. Reduce the heat, cover, and simmer for 45 minutes.
2. Heat half the oil in a large pan and stir-fry the mushrooms for 5 minutes. Remove from the pan and set aside. Add the remaining oil to the pan with the onion, garlic, potatoes, bell pepper, and spices. Fry over a medium heat for 10 minutes.
3. Drain the beans, reserving the cooking liquid. Boil the liquid until reduced to about 2 cups. Stir the beans into the pan containing the vegetables; add the reduced bean liquid, strained tomatoes, and mushrooms. Bring to a boil, cover, and simmer for 30 minutes.
4. Meanwhile, make the avocado salsa. Peel, pit, and finely dice the avocado and combine with the remaining ingredients, seasoning to taste. Cover and set aside.
5. Stir the lime juice, chocolate, and cilantro into the chili and cook for a further 5 minutes. Serve piping hot topped with a spoonful of the avocado salsa.

3

Entrées

Serves 4 / Preparation time: 15 minutes / Cooking time: about 1 hour 10 minutes / Oven temperature: 350°F

Baked Bean Cassoulet

½ cup olive oil

4 chicken thighs or drumsticks, skinned

1 pound herb sausages

½ cup chorizo or pepperoni sausage,
　thinly sliced

2 onions, thinly sliced

⅔ cup chicken stock

3 garlic cloves, crushed

several sprigs of thyme

2 x 15-ounce cans baked beans in
　tomato sauce

¼ cup Worcestershire sauce

¼ cup tomato purée

½ teaspoon ground cloves

¾ cup breadcrumbs

salt and pepper

1. Heat the oil in a large frying pan and fry the chicken pieces and herb sausages for about 10 minutes until golden. Add the chorizo or pepperoni and onions and fry for a further 2 minutes. Transfer to a casserole dish and add the stock, garlic, and thyme. Cover and bake in a preheated oven at 350°F for 30 minutes.

2. Remove from the oven and stir in the baked beans, Worcestershire sauce, tomato purée, cloves, and seasoning until evenly combined.

3. Sprinkle with the breadcrumbs and return to the oven, uncovered, for 25–30 minutes until the breadcrumbs are golden and the chicken is cooked. Serve hot.

Farmer-style Cannellini Beans

1 pound dried cannellini beans, soaked
    overnight, drained and rinsed

8½ cups water

1 celery stalk, chopped

2 bay leaves

4-ounce piece of smoked bacon

¼ cup fatback

⅓ cup extra virgin olive oil

½ onion, finely chopped

2 tablespoons chopped sage leaves

1 sprig of rosemary, plus extra to garnish

1 garlic clove, crushed

3 ripe plum tomatoes, peeled, seeded,
    and chopped

½ vegetable bouillon cube

2 tablespoons red wine

salt and pepper

1. Place the beans, water, celery, and bay leaves in a large saucepan. Bring to the boil and simmer for at least 2 hours until tender. Drain.

2. Meanwhile, place the bacon in a small saucepan with sufficient water to cover it and boil for 10 minutes. Remove with a slotted spoon and cut into bite-sized pieces.

3. Chop the fatback and place in a large shallow pan with the oil. Add the onion, herbs and garlic; cook over a medium heat until the onion is golden.

4. Add the drained cooked beans, mix together, season with salt and pepper to taste, and leave for 10 minutes to allow the flavors to mingle.

5. Add the tomatoes and boiled bacon to the beans. Crumble in the bouillon cube and stir in the red wine.

6. Leave the sauce to thicken a little, then taste and adjust the seasoning, if necessary. Serve hot, garnished with rosemary sprigs.

Serves 4 / Preparation time: 25 minutes / Cooking time: 15 minutes

Fusilli with Fava Beans, Parma Ham, and Mint

You can use any variety of dried pasta for this dish. Skinning the shelled beans is slightly laborious, but well worth the effort.

1 pound shelled fava beans

¾ pound dried fusilli or other pasta shapes

½ cup extra virgin olive oil

2 garlic cloves, finely chopped

⅔ cup dry white wine

¾ cup light cream

¼ cup chopped mint

4 slices of Parma ham, cut into thin strips

2 tablespoons Pecorino Sardo or Parmesan cheese, freshly grated, plus extra to serve

pepper

1. Blanch the beans in a large saucepan of lightly salted boiling water for 1 minute. Drain, rinse immediately under cold running water, and drain again. Carefully peel away and discard the rather tough outer skins of the beans to reveal the bright green, velvety bean inside.
2. Cook the pasta in a large saucepan of lightly salted boiling water according to package instructions, until al dente.
3. Meanwhile, heat the oil in a deep frying pan and gently fry the garlic until softened, but not browned. Add the wine and boil rapidly until it is reduced to about ¼ cup; then stir in the cream, mint, and season with pepper and heat through.
4. Drain the pasta and add to the sauce with the beans, the Parma ham, and Pecorino Sardo or Parmesan. Stir over the heat for about 30 seconds and serve with extra cheese.

Tagliatelle with Borlotti Beans

1. Heat the oil in a large heavy-based pan; add the bacon, onion, and whole sage leaves. Cook over a medium heat until golden. Add the beans.
2. Mix the flour and tomato purée in a small bowl, then stir in the stock and wine. Pour into the bean mixture, stir with a wooden spoon, and simmer over a low heat until the sauce thickens.
3. Meanwhile, cook the pasta in a large saucepan of lightly salted boiling water according to package instructions, until al dente.
4. Remove the sage leaves from the sauce and discard. Taste the sauce and adjust the seasoning, if necessary. Drain the pasta, mix with the sauce and tip into a large, warm serving platter. Add the Parmesan and pecorino and serve hot, garnished with sprigs of sage.

⅓ cup extra virgin olive oil

3-ounce piece of smoked bacon, cubed

1 onion, finely chopped

5 sage leaves

1 cup canned borlotti or cranberry beans,
   drained and rinsed

½ tablespoon all-purpose flour

2 tablespoons tomato purée

¼ cup hot chicken stock

¼ cup red wine

¾ pound dried or fresh tagliatelle

¼ cup grated Parmesan cheese

2 tablespoons grated pecorino cheese

salt and pepper

4 sprigs of sage, to garnish

FOOD FACT

Cranberry beans, also called shell beans, have
a nutlike flavor. They have large beige pods with
red splotches and cream-colored insides
streaked with red. They are available fresh or
dried and must be shelled before cooking.

Italian Sausages and Beans with Sage

The Italian name for this dish is *salsiccie con fagioli all'uccelletto*. *Uccelletto* is Italian for a small bird such as a thrush or lark, and the Tuscan term *all'uccelletto* is used to describe this bean dish because it is flavored with sage, a herb often used when cooking small birds.

2 cups dried cannellini beans, soaked overnight, drained, and rinsed

⅔ cup extra virgin olive oil

1 pound fresh Italian pork sausages, chopped

1 cup strained tomatoes

2 garlic cloves, crushed

1 sprig of fresh sage or 2 teaspoons dried sage

salt and pepper

sage leaves, to garnish

1. Place the beans in a large saucepan, cover with fresh cold water and bring to a boil. Boil rapidly for 10 minutes, then reduce the heat and half cover with a lid. Simmer for 1¼ hours, or until the beans are tender, skimming off the scum and adding more water as necessary.
2. Drain the beans and reserve the cooking liquid.
3. Heat ⅓ cup of the oil in a flameproof casserole or heavy-based saucepan. Add the sausages and cook over a medium heat until browned on all sides. Add the tomatoes, garlic, sage, and salt and pepper to taste, and stir well to mix. Bring to a boil, then add the beans and a few spoonfuls of the cooking liquid. Cover and simmer, stirring frequently, for 15 minutes—the consistency should be quite thick. Adjust the seasoning to taste.
4. Just before serving, drizzle the remaining olive oil over the dish and garnish with sage leaves.

FOOD FACT

There are many different types of Italian fresh pork sausages (*salsiccie puro suino*). They can vary from mild to herby or spicy-hot in flavor; most have a high meat content. Visit an Italian delicatessen for the best choice. *Salsiccie a metro* is a long thin sausage, traditionally sold by the meter, although now more often sold by weight. *Luganega*, a variety of *salsiccie a metro*, and *salamelle*, which is sold in links, are both suitable for this recipe.

Serves 4–6 / Preparation time: 15 minutes, plus overnight soaking / Cooking time: 3½–4½ hours / Oven temperature: 300°F

Campfire Bean Pot

1 pound dried navy beans, soaked overnight

2 tablespoons soft brown sugar

¼ teaspoon ground cinnamon

2 teaspoons mustard powder

½ cup molasses

1 large onion, chopped

2 garlic cloves, crushed

4 tomatoes, peeled and chopped

1 sprig of thyme

1 bay leaf

2 whole cloves

12-ounce piece of rindless bacon

⅓ cup dark rum (optional)

salt and pepper

To serve:

corn on the cob

hot dogs

1. Drain the beans, rinse well, and place in a large flameproof casserole. In a small bowl, mix together the sugar, cinnamon, mustard, and molasses, then add to the beans. Add the remaining ingredients, except the rum, pushing the bacon down into the center of the beans.

2. Pour over water to cover, about 2½ cups, bring to the boil, cover the casserole with a tight-fitting lid and place in a preheated oven at 300°F for 3–4 hours. Check occasionally and top up with boiling water if it seems too dry.

3. Stir in the rum, if using, and adjust the seasoning to taste. Remove the bacon, slice it and place the slices on top of the casserole. Return to the oven and cook uncovered for 20–30 minutes. Serve with corn on the cob and hot dogs.

**Serves 4 / Preparation time: 15 minutes, plus marinating / Cooking time: 1¾ hours /
Oven temperature: 350°F**

Chinese Chicken with Black Beans

1. Soak the salted black beans in cold water for 20 minutes; drain well and set aside.
2. Meanwhile, mix the marinade ingredients together, with pepper to taste, and use to coat the chicken inside and out. Place the chicken in a roasting bag, tie loosely and place in a roasting pan. Leave to marinate for 4–6 hours, then make several holes in the bag, following the manufacturer's instructions.
3. Cook the chicken in a preheated oven at 350°F, for 1¼ hours. Remove the chicken from the bag, reserving the juices, and place it in the roasting pan. Increase the oven temperature to 400°F and cook for a further 25–30 minutes, until the juices run clear.
4. Meanwhile, heat the vegetable and sesame oils in a pan, add the scallions and stir-fry over a high heat for 30 seconds. Add the chilies and drained black beans and cook for 2 minutes. Skim off as much fat as possible from the reserved contents of the roasting bag, add the remaining liquid to the pan with the sherry and sugar. Blend the cornstarch with the water and stir into the mixture; cook until clear and syrupy.
5. Carve the chicken and serve on warm plates. Pour the black bean sauce over the chicken slices and garnish with scallion fans and red bell pepper strips.

¼ cup salted black beans

3-pound roasting chicken

2 tablespoons vegetable oil

1 teaspoon dark sesame oil

6 scallions, diagonally sliced

1–2 red chilies, seeded and thinly sliced

⅓ cup dry sherry

1 teaspoon sugar

2 tablespoons cornstarch

⅓ cup water

Marinade:

2 tablespoons fresh ginger, peeled and
   coarsely grated

¼ cup soy sauce

pepper

To garnish:

scallion fans (see Tip)

strips of red bell pepper

TIP

To make scallion fans, trim the tops off the scallions and remove the root base. Carefully slit both ends of each onion lengthwise, leaving the middle section of the onion intact. Leave in a bowl of iced water until the scallions have opened up into "fan" shapes.

**Serves 4–6 / Preparation time: 30 minutes, plus overnight soaking /
Cooking time: 2½ hours / Oven temperature: 325°F**

Lamb, Navy Bean, and Endive Casserole with a Breadcrumb Topping

2 cups dried navy beans, soaked overnight,
   drained, and rinsed

¼ cup extra virgin olive oil

4 pounds boneless leg or shoulder of lamb,
   trimmed and cut into 1½-inch cubes

1 large red or white onion, sliced

2 whole garlic cloves

1¾ cup ripe tomatoes, peeled and chopped

¼ cup tomato purée

1 sprig of rosemary

3 endive or radicchio heads, sliced into ½-inch
   strips, core removed

salt and pepper

parsley, to garnish

Breadcrumb topping:

1 cup fresh white breadcrumbs

⅓ cup extra virgin olive oil

¼ cup chopped flat leaf parsley

¼ cup finely grated Parmesan cheese

salt and pepper

1. Place the navy beans in a saucepan with enough water to cover. Bring to a boil, reduce the heat, and simmer for 30 minutes; then drain.
2. Meanwhile, heat the olive oil in a large flameproof casserole over a moderate heat. Add the lamb, in batches, and brown well all over. Remove the browned meat with a slotted spoon and set aside.
3. Reduce the heat under the casserole, add the onion and garlic, and cook gently for 8–10 minutes until softened. Add the tomatoes, tomato purée, and rosemary together with the reserved meat and the cooked beans, and add enough water to cover—about 2½ cups. Bring to a boil, season, cover with a tight-fitting lid, and place in a preheated oven at 325°F for 1½ hours.
4. Mix the topping ingredients together and season with salt and pepper. Remove the lid from the casserole, taste and adjust the seasoning, then sprinkle over the sliced endive and the breadcrumb topping. Return the casserole to the oven for 20–30 minutes until the meat is tender and the topping is golden. Serve hot, garnished with parsley.

Lamb, Artichoke, and Fava Bean Tagine

FOOD FACT

Artichokes in oil (which are now sold by many supermarkets) have a much better flavor and texture than canned artichokes. The oil left from the artichokes can be used in cooking, for tossing with pasta, rice, or pulses and making salad dressings. If you can't get artichokes in oil, canned artichokes can be substituted but be sure to rinse them after draining.

pinch of saffron threads

¼ cup hot water

1 bunch of parsley

1 bunch of cilantro

⅓ cup olive oil or oil from the artichokes (see Food Fact)

3 pounds leg or shoulder of lamb, cut into large chunks

1 onion, sliced

2 garlic cloves, crushed

1 cup stock or water

1 teaspoon ground coriander

1 teaspoon ground ginger

1 x 1-pound jar artichokes in oil, drained

1 pound frozen fava beans, thawed

2 Preserved Lemons (see page 20), rinds only, diced

pepper

cilantro sprigs, to garnish

durum wheat grains (blé) or couscous, to serve

1. Soak the saffron in the hot water. Tie the bunches of parsley and cilantro together with kitchen string.

2. Heat the oil in a flameproof casserole. Add the lamb in batches and fry until evenly browned. Place on paper towels to drain.

3. Stir the onion into the casserole and cook until softened and lightly browned, adding the garlic when the onion is almost ready. Return the meat to the casserole then pour in the stock or water and add the coriander, ginger, saffron, and bunches of herbs. Cover the casserole tightly and cook gently, stirring occasionally, for about 1¼ hours or until the lamb is just tender.

4. Stir the artichokes, fava beans, and preserved lemon rinds into the casserole, cover and cook for a further 30 minutes. To serve, discard the bunches of herbs, season to taste and garnish with cilantro. Serve with grains or couscous.

New Mexican Beef and Bean Stew with Corn Dumplings

3 cups dried red or black kidney beans, soaked
overnight, drained, and rinsed

¼ cup extra virgin olive oil

1½ pounds boneless shin of beef, cut into
1-inch cubes

1 large onion, chopped

2–3 garlic cloves, crushed

2 teaspoons ground cumin

2 teaspoons ground coriander

2–3 large red chilies, roasted, peeled, seeded,
and finely chopped (see Tip)

1 bay leaf

1 sprig of thyme

2 large tomatoes, skinned and
chopped

2½ cups beef stock

¾ cup chopped cilantro

salt

Cornmeal dumplings:

⅔ cup all-purpose flour

⅓ cup fine cornmeal

1½ teaspoons superfine sugar

1 teaspoon baking powder

¼ teaspoon salt

⅓ cup buttermilk, at room temperature

1 egg, beaten

2 tablespoons unsalted butter,
melted

½ cup canned corn kernels, drained

1. Boil the beans vigorously in a large saucepan of unsalted water for 10 minutes; then drain.
2. Heat the oil in a large flameproof casserole. Add the meat in batches and brown well all over. Remove the browned meat with a slotted spoon and set aside.
3. Add the onion and garlic to the casserole and cook until the onion is golden brown, then add the cumin and ground coriander and cook for 1–2 minutes.
4. Add the drained beans, the meat, and all the remaining ingredients except the cilantro and salt, and just enough water to cover—about 1¼ cups. Bring to a boil, reduce the heat, cover tightly, and simmer for 2–2½ hours until the meat is tender.
5. To make the dumplings, sift together the flour, cornmeal, sugar, baking powder, and salt into a bowl. Add the buttermilk, egg, and butter and stir until combined, then gently stir in the corn.
6. Stir the cilantro into the stew and season with salt. Drop 12 spoonfuls of the dumpling mixture over the stew, replace the lid and cook for 10–15 minutes until the dumplings are light and cooked. Serve hot.

TIP

To roast chilies, place them on a baking sheet and cook under a preheated broiler for about 5–10 minutes, turning occasionally until well charred and blistered all over. Remove from the heat and place in a plastic bag. Close the bag and leave the chilies to cool—the steam produced in the bag will help in removing the chili skins. When cool enough to handle, peel off the skin and remove the membranes and seeds. Chop the chilies as needed.

Serves 4 / Preparation time: 5 minutes / Cooking time: 1–1¼ hours

Chili con Carne

One of the Southwest's best-known dishes, this recipe combines beef, beans, and fiery chilies to splendid effect.

¼ cup oil

3 onions, chopped

1 red bell pepper, cored, seeded, and diced

1 green bell pepper, cored, seeded, and diced

2 garlic cloves, crushed

1 pound lean ground beef

2 cups beef stock

¼–1 tablespoon chili powder

2 cups cooked kidney beans

1 x 14.5-ounce can chopped tomatoes

1 teaspoon ground cumin

salt and pepper

parsley, to garnish

To serve:

soft flour tortillas

sour cream

pickled green chilies

grated Cheddar cheese (optional)

1. Heat the oil in a heavy-based saucepan or flameproof casserole. Add the onions, bell peppers, and garlic and gently fry until soft. Add the meat and fry until just colored. Blend in the stock and add the chili powder, beans, tomatoes, and cumin. Season with salt and pepper.

2. Bring to a boil, then cover, reduce the heat, and simmer very gently for 50–60 minutes, stirring occasionally.

3. Serve the chili wrapped in soft flour tortillas, garnished with parsley and accompanied by the sour cream, green chilies, and grated cheese, if liked.

4 Salads

Lobia Salad

Black-eyed peas feature in this unusual salad.

2 potatoes, finely diced

1 cup green beans, trimmed and cut into 1-inch
   lengths

1 x 15-ounce can black-eyed peas, drained and
   rinsed

4 scallions, thinly sliced

1 green chili, seeded, and finely chopped

1 tomato, roughly chopped

handful of mint leaves

warm naan bread, to serve

Dressing:

¼ cup light olive oil

2 tablespoons lemon juice

1 teaspoon chili powder

1 teaspoon clear honey

salt and pepper

1. Cook the potatoes and green beans in a large saucepan of lightly salted boiling water for 8–10 minutes. Drain and place in a large serving bowl.

2. Add the black-eyed peas, scallions, green chili, tomato, and mint leaves. Toss well to mix.

3. Combine all the dressing ingredients in a small bowl or screw-top jar and mix well. Pour over the salad, mix well, and serve with warm naan bread.

Arugula, Tuna, and Navy Bean Salad

4 tomatoes, peeled, cored, and roughly chopped

2 cups arugula

1 x 15-ounce can navy beans, rinsed and drained

1 x 6-ounce can tuna in olive oil

1 red onion, chopped

⅔ cup artichoke hearts in olive oil

2 young celery stalks with leaves, chopped

2 tablespoons pitted black olives

½ cup lemon juice

2 tablespoons red wine vinegar

¼ teaspoon dried chili flakes

handful of flat leaf parsley, roughly chopped

salt and pepper

warm crusty bread, to serve

1. Place the tomatoes in a large salad bowl with the arugula.
2. Stir in the navy beans and the tuna and its olive oil, roughly breaking up the tuna into large flakes. Stir in the red onion.
3. Add the artichoke hearts and their olive oil, the celery, olives, lemon juice, red wine vinegar, dried chili flakes, and parsley and season with salt and pepper.
4. Mix all the ingredients together well and allow to stand for 30 minutes for the flavors to mingle. Serve at room temperature with warm crusty bread.

Serves 4 / Preparation time: 10 minutes / Cooking time: 2 minutes

Tomato and Green Bean Salad

2 cups mixed red and yellow baby tomatoes
(plum tomatoes if possible)
2 cups thin green beans, trimmed
handful of mint, chopped
1 garlic clove, crushed
½ cup extra virgin olive oil
2 tablespoons balsamic vinegar
salt and pepper

1. Cut the baby tomatoes in half and place in a large bowl.
2. Blanch the green beans in a saucepan of lightly salted boiling water for 2 minutes, then drain well and place in the bowl with the tomatoes.
3. Add the chopped mint, garlic, olive oil, and balsamic vinegar. Season with salt and pepper and mix well. Serve warm or cold.

FOOD FACT
Balsamic vinegar is a dark brown, rich, concentrated, sweet vinegar made from the must of white grapes. Traditionally from Modena in Italy, true balsamic vinegar is aged in wooden barrels and can be quite expensive. Use it sparingly in salads or in cooking.

Serves 4 / Preparation time: 10 minutes / Cooking time: 2 minutes

White Bean and Sun-dried Tomato Salad

¼ cup olive oil

1 garlic clove, crushed

1 x 15-ounce can cannellini beans, drained
and rinsed

1 red onion, sliced

½ cup sun-dried tomatoes in oil, drained and
roughly chopped

2 tablespoons chopped black olives

2 teaspoons chopped capers

2 teaspoons chopped thyme

2 tablespoons parsley leaves

2 tablespoons extra virgin olive oil

¼ cup lemon juice

salt and pepper

1. Heat the oil in a frying pan. Add the
garlic and sauté over a high heat, stirring,
to get a little color. When it is golden,
remove from the pan.

2. Place the beans in a mixing bowl and stir
in the garlic. Add the onion, sun-dried
tomatoes, olives, capers, thyme, parsley,
extra virgin olive oil, lemon juice, and salt
and pepper to taste; mix well. Check the
seasoning and serve.

FOOD FACT

Capers are the small, green, unopened flower
buds of a Mediterranean shrub. They are used,
pickled, as a flavoring and as a garnish and
are an essential ingredient in both Italian and
Provençal cooking. They have a characteristic
slightly bitter flavor, which is developed
by pickling.

Serves 4 / Preparation time: 10 minutes / Cooking time: 2 minutes

New Season Fava Bean and Pecorino Salad

3 cups shelled fresh fava beans

1½ cups pecorino cheese, coarsely grated

¼ cup extra virgin olive oil

¼ cup lemon juice

2 tablespoons chopped flat leaf parsley

salt and pepper

1. Blanch the beans in a saucepan of lightly salted boiling water for 2 minutes. Drain, rinse immediately under cold running water, and drain again. If you have the time after blanching the beans, carefully peel away and discard the rather tough outer skins to reveal the bright green, velvety bean inside.

2. Place the cheese in a mixing bowl. Just before serving, add the beans, olive oil, lemon juice, and parsley, season with salt and pepper and mix well.

**Serves 4 / Preparation time: 10 minutes, plus overnight soaking and standing /
Cooking time: 45 minutes / Oven temperature: 325°F**

Cannellini Bean Salad

White, kidney-shaped cannellini beans feature in central Italian cooking, whereas rosy borlotti beans tend to appear in recipes from northern and southern Italy. The flavor is at its height if the beans are tossed while hot and eaten while still warm, so try to time the cooking of the beans so that they can stand for 1 hour between dressing and serving. For the best flavor and texture, buy Italian beans from a good Italian deli.

2 cups dried cannellini beans, soaked overnight,
    drained, and rinsed

⅓ cup extra virgin olive oil

2–3 anchovy fillets, rinsed if necessary

yolks of 2 hard-boiled eggs

2 tablespoons coarsely chopped onion

2 tablespoons white wine vinegar or lemon juice

3 sage leaves

¼ cup coarsely chopped parsley

salt and pepper

1. Place the beans in a heavy-based flameproof casserole with just enough water to cover. Bring to a boil then cook over a medium heat for 10 minutes; cover and cook in a preheated oven at 325°F for 30 minutes, until tender. Keep an eye on the level of the water and pour in a little more if the beans become too dry, but there should be hardly any water left at the end of the cooking time.
2. Purée the olive oil, anchovies, egg yolks, onion, vinegar, or lemon juice, herbs, and salt and pepper to taste in a blender or food processor.
3. Drain the cannellini beans and place in a large bowl. Pour the dressing over them and toss gently until the beans are well coated. Leave at room temperature for 1 hour, then toss again just before serving.

VARIATION

Tuscan *Fagioli all'Uccelletto*: Cook 3 cups soaked and drained cannellini beans as above. Fry 5 sage leaves and 2 crushed garlic cloves in ⅓ cup extra virgin olive oil in a shallow earthenware dish until the garlic begins to color. Stir in the beans and cook for about 5 minutes before adding 1 pound well-flavored tomatoes, peeled, seeded, and chopped, and salt and pepper. Cover and cook over a moderate heat for about 20 minutes.

**Serves 4 / Preparation time: 15 minutes /
Cooking time: 40 minutes / Oven temperature: 400°F**

Flageolet Bean and Roasted Vegetable Salad

1 eggplant, trimmed

1 red bell pepper, halved, cored, and seeded

1 yellow bell pepper, halved, cored, and seeded

1 zucchini, trimmed

4 garlic cloves, peeled but left whole

½ cup extra virgin olive oil

1 teaspoon coarse sea salt

2½ cups cooked flageolet or navy beans

¼ cup chopped mixed herbs (such as parsley and
    oregano and mint)

¾ cup vinaigrette dressing

pepper

mint leaves, to garnish

1. Cut all the vegetables into strips and place in a roasting pan. Add the garlic cloves. Sprinkle with the olive oil, sea salt, and pepper.

2. Place in a preheated oven at 400°F and roast for 40 minutes. Transfer to a shallow bowl and leave to cool.

3. Add the beans and toss lightly. Stir the herbs into the vinaigrette dressing; pour over the salad and serve garnished with mint.

Bean and Rice Salad

¾ cup dried red kidney beans, soaked overnight, drained, and rinsed

½ cup dried cannellini beans, soaked overnight, drained, and rinsed

¾ cup brown rice

1 small onion, finely chopped

½ cup raisins

½ cup cashews, roasted

½ red bell pepper, cored, seeded, and cut into diamonds

¼ cup chopped parsley

salt and pepper

lemon wedges, to serve

sprigs of flat leaf parsley, to garnish

Dressing:

⅓ cup sunflower oil

¼ cup soy sauce

2 tablespoons lemon juice

1 garlic clove, crushed

salt and pepper

1. Place the kidney beans and the cannellini beans separately in 2 large saucepans with plenty of cold water. Bring to a boil over a high heat and boil for 15 minutes. Reduce the heat, cover, and simmer for 1–1½ hours adding a little salt toward the end of cooking time. Drain and cool.

2. Meanwhile, cook the rice in a saucepan of lightly salted boiling water for 40–45 minutes until tender. Rinse, drain well, and allow to cool.

3. Place the beans and rice in a large mixing bowl and stir in the onion, raisins, cashews, red bell pepper, and parsley. Season with salt and pepper.

4. Place all the dressing ingredients in a screw-top jar and shake until well blended. Season with salt and pepper. Pour over the rice and beans and stir well.

5. Transfer to a serving bowl and serve with lemon wedges and sprigs of parsley.

Marinated Zucchini and Bean Salad

2 cups green beans, trimmed and cut into
  1-inch lengths

3 cups zucchini, diced

1 x 15-ounce canned black-eyed peas, drained
  and rinsed

¼ cup extra virgin olive oil

¼ cup lemon juice

1 garlic clove, crushed

¼ cup chopped parsley

salt and pepper

toasted slices of crusty bread, to serve (optional)

1. Cook the green beans in a large saucepan of lightly salted boiling water for 5 minutes. Add the zucchini and cook for a further 5 minutes. Drain thoroughly and place in a bowl with the black-eyed peas.

2. Add the remaining ingredients, with salt and pepper to taste, while the vegetables are warm and mix well to combine. Leave to cool and serve with toasted slices of crusty bread, if desired.

Serves 4 / Preparation time: 10 minutes / Cooking time: 11 minutes

Smoked Tuna and Bean Salad

Smoked tuna is available in cans at delis and specialty stores. The more traditional canned tuna can be used, but buy tuna packed in olive oil.

½ pound baby new potatoes

1 cup fine green beans, trimmed

2 x 4-ounce cans smoked tuna in olive oil, drained and flaked

1 x 15-ounce can borlotti beans or cranberry beans, drained and rinsed

4 ripe plum tomatoes, roughly chopped

½ cup Niçoise olives

¼ cup capers in brine, drained and rinsed

Dressing:

2 sun-dried tomatoes in oil, drained and roughly chopped

1 small garlic clove, crushed

½ teaspoon dried oregano

2 tablespoons white wine vinegar

pinch of sugar

¾ cup extra virgin olive oil

salt and pepper

1. Cook the potatoes in a saucepan of lightly salted boiling water for 8 minutes. Add the green beans and cook for a further 3 minutes, until both the potatoes and beans are tender. Drain, rinse immediately under cold running water, and drain again, then pat dry and place in a large bowl.

2. Add the tuna, canned beans, tomatoes, olives, and capers to the bowl.

3. To make the dressing, put the sun-dried tomatoes, garlic, oregano, vinegar, sugar, and olive oil in a blender or food processor and process to a purée. Season to taste with salt and pepper. Pour the dressing over the salad, toss well, and serve.

5 More Than Beans

Serves 4 / Preparation time: 10 minutes / Cooking time: 25–30 minutes

Green Lentil Soup with Spiced Butter

Serve the spicy butter separately for stirring into the soup, so that each person can spice up their own portion according to personal taste.

¼ cup extra virgin olive oil

2 onions, chopped

2 bay leaves

green lentils, rinsed

4½ cups Vegetable Stock (see page 21)

½ teaspoon ground turmeric

small handful of cilantro leaves, roughly chopped

salt and pepper

Spiced butter:

¼ cup lightly salted butter, softened

1 large garlic clove, crushed

2 tablespoons chopped cilantro

1 teaspoon paprika

1 teaspoon cumin seeds

1 red chili, seeded, and finely chopped

1. Heat the oil in a saucepan. Add the onions and sauté for 3 minutes. Add the bay leaves, lentils, vegetable stock, and turmeric. Bring to a boil, then reduce the heat, cover, and simmer for 20 minutes, or until the lentils are tender and turning mushy.

2. Meanwhile, to make the spiced butter, beat the butter with the garlic, cilantro, paprika, cumin seeds, and chili and transfer to a small serving dish.

3. Stir the cilantro leaves into the soup, season to taste with salt and pepper, and serve with the spiced butter in a separate bowl at the table for stirring into the soup.

Chickpea Soup

Instead of serving this as a chunky soup, it can
be puréed and served with a little extra virgin
olive oil swirled into each serving.

½ cup extra virgin olive oil

1 onion, chopped

3 garlic cloves, crushed

2 tablespoons paprika

2 tablespoons ground coriander

2 teaspoons ground cumin

2 sprigs of thyme

pinch of dried chili flakes

2 cups dried chickpeas, soaked overnight,
   drained and rinsed

6¼ cups Vegetable Stock (see page 21)

1 large potato, chopped

2 carrots, sliced

2 celery stalks, sliced

3 tomatoes, chopped

⅓ cup chopped cilantro, plus extra to garnish

salt and pepper

1. Heat the oil in a saucepan. Add the onion and garlic and fry for 5–7 minutes until softened and beginning to brown. Add the paprika, ground coriander, and cumin and stir for 2 minutes.

2. Add the thyme, dried chili flakes, chickpeas, and vegetable stock. Bring to a boil then cover the pan and simmer the soup for 40 minutes.

3. Add the potato, carrots, celery, tomatoes, and cilantro to the pan. Cover and simmer for a further 30–40 minutes until the chickpeas and vegetables are tender.

4. Season to taste with salt and pepper and serve with more cilantro scattered over the top.

Serves 6 / Preparation time: 10 minutes / Cooking time: 50 minutes

Split Pea Soup

3¾ cups yellow or green split peas, rinsed
1 large onion, chopped
2 garlic cloves, crushed
3 large sprigs of mint
⅓ cup extra virgin olive oil
salt and pepper

Spiced butter:
2 garlic cloves, crushed
2 scallions, finely chopped
1 teaspoon ground coriander
small pinch of dried chili flakes
small handful of cilantro leaves, chopped
¼ cup chopped mint
¼ cup unsalted butter

FOOD FACT

Split peas are usually yellow or green. They do not require soaking before use and easily cook to a purée (green split peas cooked to a purée are the basis of the traditional English dish, pease pudding). Ham or smoked pork chops are classic partners when cooking split peas.

1. Place the split peas, onion, garlic, sprigs of mint, and olive oil in a large saucepan. Add enough water to cover generously and bring to a boil.
2. Reduce the heat, cover the pan, and simmer for about 35 minutes, or until the split peas are very tender. Remove the lid toward the end of cooking if necessary— the split peas should be just covered with water.
3. Meanwhile, make the spiced butter. Place all the ingredients for the butter in a bowl and crush to a paste. Cover and store in the refrigerator until required.
4. Transfer two-thirds of the split peas and their liquid to a blender or food processor, purée until smooth then return to the pan. Simmer for a few minutes until thickened to the desired consistency, then season to taste with salt and pepper.
5. Serve the soup in warm bowls with a knob of the spiced butter floating on top.

Serves 6 / Preparation time: 15–20 minutes, plus overnight soaking / Cooking time: about 1¼ hours

Lamb Soup with Chickpeas and Couscous

1½ teaspoons cumin seeds

1½ teaspoons coriander seeds

¼ cup extra virgin olive oil

6 ounces lean lamb, finely chopped

1 large onion, chopped

3 garlic cloves, crushed

1 red chili, seeded and finely chopped

1½ teaspoons ground allspice

1 x 28-ounce can chopped tomatoes

¼ cup tomato purée

3⅓ cups Vegetable Stock (see
   page 21)

1 cup dried chickpeas, soaked overnight,
   drained, and rinsed

¼ cup chopped parsley

2 tablespoons chopped mint

½ cup couscous

about 2 teaspoons sugar

salt and pepper

lemon wedges, to serve

1. Place the cumin and coriander seeds in a small, heavy-based frying pan and dry-fry over a moderate heat, stirring, for 1–2 minutes until fragrant—do not let them burn. Leave to cool, then grind to a powder in a spice grinder or using a pestle and mortar. Alternatively, put them in a small bowl and crush them with the end of a rolling pin. Set aside.

2. Heat the oil in a large heavy-based saucepan. Add the lamb to the pan and brown quickly. Using a slotted spoon, remove the lamb and place on paper towels to drain. Stir the onion into the pan and cook until soft and browned, adding the garlic and chili when the onion is almost cooked.

3. Add the dry-roasted and crushed cumin and coriander seeds and the allspice and stir for 1 minute.

4. Return the lamb to the pan and add the canned tomatoes, tomato purée, stock, and chickpeas. Stir well, then cover the pan and simmer very gently for about 1 hour until the chickpeas are tender.

5. Stir the parsley, mint, and couscous into the soup, cover, and remove from the heat. Add the sugar and salt and pepper to taste. Serve accompanied by lemon wedges.

Lentil, Eggplant, and Coconut Dhal

This creamy, mildly spiced dhal makes a delicious accompaniment to Indian curries.

¾ cup red split lentils, rinsed
1 teaspoon ground turmeric
2 cinnamon sticks
3 cups hot Vegetable Stock
  (see page 21)
½ cup sunflower oil
4 red chilies, seeded and chopped
2 garlic cloves, crushed
2 teaspoons fenugreek seeds
1 teaspoon yellow mustard seeds
1 large onion, chopped
1 eggplant, diced
2 teaspoons garam masala
¼ cup tomato purée
2 tablespoons lemon juice
½ cup coconut milk
¼ cup chopped cilantro
salt and pepper

To garnish:
plain yogurt
chopped cilantro

1. Place the lentils in a saucepan with the turmeric, cinnamon sticks, and hot stock. Bring to a boil, cover, and simmer for 35–40 minutes until the lentils are softened and most of the stock has been absorbed.

2. Meanwhile, heat 2 tablespoons of the oil in a frying pan. Add the chilies, garlic, fenugreek seeds, and mustard seeds and fry for 5 minutes until golden. Remove from the pan and set aside, reserving a teaspoon of the spice mixture for garnish.

3. Add the remaining oil to the frying pan and fry the onion and eggplant for 10 minutes until golden.

4. Return the chili mixture to the pan with the garam masala, lentils, tomato purée, and lemon juice. Simmer for 5 minutes. Meanwhile, mix together the yogurt, cilantro, and reserved spice mixture for the garnish.

5. Stir the coconut milk into the dhal until it dissolves and add the cilantro; season to taste and serve at once topped with a spoonful of the yogurt garnish.

Braised Lentils with Mushrooms and Gremolata

Gremolata is a blend of chopped garlic, parsley, and lemon zest, which gives a delicious lift to soups and stews. Sprinkle it on before serving.

¼ cup butter

1 onion, chopped

2 celery stalks, sliced

2 carrots, sliced

1 cup Puy lentils, rinsed

1½ cups Vegetable Stock (see page 21)

1 cup dry white wine

2 bay leaves

¼ cup chopped thyme

⅓ cup extra virgin olive oil

3 cups mushrooms, sliced

salt and pepper

Gremolata:

¼ cup chopped parsley

finely grated zest of 1 lemon

2 garlic cloves, chopped

1. Melt the butter in a saucepan. Add the onion, celery, and carrots and sauté for 3 minutes. Add the lentils, vegetable stock, wine, herbs, and a little salt and pepper. Bring to a boil, then reduce the heat and simmer gently, uncovered, for about 20 minutes, or until the lentils are tender.
2. Meanwhile, mix together the ingredients for the gremolata.
3. Heat the oil in a frying pan. Add the mushrooms and sauté quickly for about 2 minutes until golden. Season lightly with salt and pepper.
4. Spoon the lentils onto 4 warm plates, top with the mushrooms, and serve, sprinkled with the gremolata.

Serves 4 / Preparation time: 10 minutes / Cooking time: 25 minutes

Mushroom and Chickpea Curry with Aromatic Rice

¼ cup butter

1 onion, chopped

2 garlic cloves, crushed

1-inch piece of fresh ginger, peeled and grated

2 cups button mushrooms

¼ cup hot curry powder

1 teaspoon ground coriander

1 teaspoon ground cinnamon

½ teaspoon turmeric

3 cups potatoes, diced

1 x 15-ounce can chickpeas, drained and rinsed

½ cup cashews, toasted and chopped (optional)

½ cup Greek or plain yogurt

chopped cilantro

salt and pepper

Aromatic rice:

1½ cups long grain rice

12 dried curry leaves

3 cardamom pods, crushed

1 cinnamon stick, crushed

1 teaspoon salt

3 cups water

1. First cook the rice. Place the rice in a saucepan with the curry leaves, spices, and salt. Add the water, bring to a boil, then cover and cook over a low heat for 10 minutes. Remove the pan from the heat, but leave the rice undisturbed for a further 10 minutes.

2. Meanwhile, melt the butter in a frying pan and fry the onion, garlic, ginger, and mushrooms for 5 minutes.

3. Add the curry powder, ground coriander, cinnamon, turmeric and potatoes, stir, then add the chickpeas. Season to taste with salt and pepper and add just enough water to cover. Bring to a boil, cover, and simmer gently for 15 minutes.

4. Stir the cashews, if using, into the curry, along with the yogurt and chopped cilantro. Heat through without boiling and serve with the rice.

Spinach and Chickpea Sabzi

This quick and tasty Indian dish uses spinach and canned chickpeas,
flavored with amchur (dried mango powder).

2 tablespoons vegetable oil

1 teaspoon cumin seeds

½ teaspoon coarsely ground coriander seeds

1 small onion, finely chopped

4 cups baby spinach

1 x 7-ounce can chopped tomatoes

1 teaspoon chili powder

2 tablespoons dhana jeera (see Food Fact)

1 teaspoon amchur

1 teaspoon light brown sugar

2 tablespoons fresh lime juice

1 x 15-ounce can chickpeas, drained and rinsed

¾ cup water

sea salt and pepper

1. Heat the oil in a large frying pan and, when hot, add the cumin and coriander seeds and the onion. Stir-fry until the onion is soft and light brown, then add the spinach and tomatoes and stir well.

2. Add the chili powder, dhana jeera, amchur, sugar, and lime juice and stir. Cook for 1–2 minutes, then add the chickpeas and water. Season with salt and pepper, cover, and simmer gently for 10 minutes, stirring occasionally. Serve hot.

FOOD FACT

Dhana jeera is a spice mixture made of
equal quantities of ground coriander and
ground cumin.

**Serves 4 as a side dish/ Preparation time: 15 minutes, plus overnight soaking /
Cooking time: 1 hour 20 minutes**

Spicy Chickpeas

2¼ cups dried chickpeas, soaked overnight,
    drained and rinsed

1½ teaspoons salt

1 whole onion, peeled, plus 2 onions, chopped

6 slices of bacon, chopped

1 garlic clove, crushed

1 red bell pepper, cored, seeded, and chopped

¼ teaspoon pepper

1 small, dried hot red chili, crumbled

½ teaspoon dried oregano

1½ cups tomatoes, peeled, seeded
    and chopped

¼ cup tomato purée

½ cup water

oregano leaves, to garnish

1. Place the chickpeas in a saucepan with 1 teaspoon of the salt and the whole onion. Cover with cold water.

2. Bring to a boil, then boil hard for 10 minutes. Reduce the heat and simmer, uncovered, for about 45 minutes, until the chickpeas are cooked and tender. Drain and set aside; discard the onion.

3. Place the bacon in a frying pan and fry until the fat starts to render. Add the chopped onions, the garlic, and red bell pepper and continue frying until soft. Stir in the remaining salt, the pepper, chili, oregano, tomatoes, tomato purée, and water.

4. Add the drained chickpeas and stir well. Simmer for 10 minutes, stirring occasionally. Serve hot, garnished with oregano leaves.

Serves 6 / Preparation time: 20 minutes, plus overnight soaking and cooling / Cooking time: 1–1½ hours

Hummus

The quantities for this delicious chickpea and sesame dip are imprecise because people's tastes vary considerably, but the flavor of sesame (the tahini) should not overpower that of the chickpeas.

FOOD FACT

Tahini, or tahina, is a thick, oily, light or dark brown paste made from ground, toasted sesame seeds. It is widely used in Middle Eastern cuisine. Tahini separates on standing so stir it well before use.

2 cups dried chickpeas, soaked overnight, drained and rinsed
2–3 garlic cloves, crushed with a little salt
about 1 cup lemon juice
about ⅔ cup tahini
salt
warm pita bread, to serve

To garnish:
extra virgin olive oil
paprika
olives

1. Cook the chickpeas in a large saucepan of boiling water until soft—1–1½ hours depending on their quality and age. Drain and reserve the cooking liquid. Purée the chickpeas in a blender or food processor with a little of the cooking liquid, then press the purée through a sieve to remove the skins.

2. Beat the garlic into the chickpea purée. Stir in the lemon juice and tahini alternately, tasting before it has all been added to get the right balance of flavors. Add a little more salt, if necessary, and more of the cooking liquid to make a soft, creamy consistency. Spoon the purée into a shallow dish, cover, and leave in the refrigerator for several hours.

3. Return to room temperature before serving. Create swirls in the surface with the back of a spoon then trickle olive oil into the swirls and sprinkle lightly with paprika. Garnish with olives and serve with warm pita bread.

Serves 4 / Preparation time: 35 minutes, plus overnight soaking / Cooking time: 1–1½ hours

Chickpea, Spinach, and Pumpkin Stew with Tomato and Chili Aïoli

3 cups dried chickpeas, soaked overnight,
    drained, and rinsed

¼ cup extra virgin olive oil

1 onion, finely chopped

1 garlic clove, finely chopped

1 pound peeled pumpkin, cut into 1-inch dice

2 cups Vegetable Stock (see page 21)

1 bay leaf

pinch of saffron threads

1 pound fresh spinach, washed and trimmed

2 tablespoons cider or white wine vinegar

salt and pepper

Tomato and chili aïoli:

4–6 garlic cloves, crushed

2 egg yolks

1 red chili, roasted, seeded and chopped
    (see page 90)

¼–½ cup lemon juice

1¼ cups extra virgin olive oil

2 tablespoons sun-dried tomato purée

salt and pepper

1. Place the chickpeas in a large saucepan with sufficient water to cover—about 5 cups. Bring to a boil, reduce the heat, and simmer for ¾–1 hour, or until tender. Drain and set aside.

2. Meanwhile, to make the aïoli, place the garlic, egg yolks, and chili in a blender or food processor, add ¼ cup of the lemon juice and process briefly to mix. With the motor running, gradually add the olive oil in a thin steady stream (as if making mayonnaise), until the mixture forms a thick cream. Scrape into a serving bowl and season to taste with salt, pepper, and more lemon juice if required. Stir in the sun-dried tomato purée and set aside.

3. Heat the oil in a large flameproof casserole over a moderate heat. Add the onion and garlic and cook for 6–8 minutes until softened and lightly golden. Add the pumpkin, stock, bay leaf, saffron, and chickpeas. Season, bring to a boil, reduce the heat and simmer for 10–15 minutes until the pumpkin is tender.

4. Stir in the spinach, cover, and cook, stirring occasionally, until the spinach has just wilted. Stir in the vinegar and adjust the seasoning to taste. Remove the bay leaf. Serve in large individual bowls and pass the aïoli around to stir into each portion.

Tarka Dhal

This is the ultimate, basic Indian comfort food. Tarka is the process by which food is given the final seasoning, in this case with spiced oil, to flavor the dish. This dhal is tasty served with basmati rice, plain yogurt, and hot green mango pickle or lime pickle.

1 cup red split lentils, rinsed

3⅓ cups hot water

1 x 7-ounce can chopped tomatoes

2 green chilies, seeded and finely
    chopped (optional)

¼ teaspoon ground turmeric

2 teaspoons grated fresh ginger

½ cup chopped cilantro

sea salt and pepper

Tarka:

2 tablespoons sunflower oil

2 teaspoons black mustard seeds

1 teaspoon cumin seeds

2 garlic cloves, thinly sliced

1 dried red chili

1. Soak the lentils in enough boiling water to cover for 10 minutes. Drain and put in a large saucepan with the measured hot water. Bring to a boil over a high heat, spooning off the scum that comes to the surface. Reduce the heat and cook for 20 minutes, or until soft and tender.

2. Drain the lentils and process to a purée in a blender or food processor or using a hand-held electric mixer. Return the purée to the rinsed pan with the tomatoes, chilies, if using, turmeric, ginger, and cilantro. Season lightly with salt and pepper, return to the heat and simmer gently.

3. Meanwhile, make the tarka. Heat the oil in a smooth nonstick frying pan. When hot, add all the tarka ingredients and fry, stirring constantly, for 1–2 minutes.

4. Remove the tarka from the heat and pour onto the cooked dhal. Stir and serve hot.

Chickpea Purée with Eggs and Spiced Oil

Smooth chickpea purée, topped with fried eggs and spicy oil, makes a great snack at any time of the day. Serve any leftover purée with warm pita bread, just as you would hummus.

1 x 15-ounce can chickpeas, drained and rinsed

3 garlic cloves, sliced

½ cup tahini

½ cup milk

⅔ cup extra virgin olive oil

½ cup lemon juice

2 eggs

½ teaspoon each of cumin, coriander, and fennel seeds, lightly crushed

1 teaspoon sesame seeds

¼ teaspoon dried chili flakes

good pinch of ground turmeric

salt and pepper

cilantro leaves, to garnish

1. Place the chickpeas in a blender or food processor with the garlic, tahini, milk, ¼ cup of the oil and ⅓ cup of the lemon juice. Season to taste with salt and pepper and process until smooth, scraping the mixture from around the sides of the bowl halfway through. Transfer to a small heavy-based saucepan and heat through gently for about 3 minutes while preparing the eggs.

2. Heat another 2 tablespoons of the oil in a small frying pan and fry the eggs. Pile the chickpea purée on 2 warm serving plates and top each mound with an egg.

3. Add the remaining oil and spices to the pan and heat through gently for 1 minute. Season lightly with salt and pepper and stir in the remaining lemon juice. Pour over the eggs and serve garnished with cilantro leaves.

Serves 4–6 / Preparation time: 30 minutes, plus overnight soaking / Cooking time: 2¼ hours

Middle Eastern Beef Casserole with Chickpeas and Zucchini

⅓ cup extra virgin olive oil

3 pounds stewing beef, cut into
   1½-inch cubes

2 onions, sliced

2 garlic cloves, chopped

3 cups tomatoes, peeled and chopped

2 tablespoons tomato purée

1 teaspoon ground allspice

¾ cup dried chickpeas, soaked overnight,
   drained, and rinsed

3¾ cups water

cayenne pepper

1½ pounds zucchini, sliced

2 tablespoons flat leaf parsley, chopped

salt and pepper

bulgur wheat, to serve

1. Heat the oil in a large flameproof casserole over a moderate heat. Add the meat, in batches, and brown well all over. Remove the browned meat using a slotted spoon and set aside.

2. Reduce the heat under the casserole, add the onions and garlic and cook for 5–6 minutes until softened. Return the meat to the pan and add the tomatoes, tomato purée, allspice, and chickpeas. Cover with the water, stir well, and bring to a boil. Season with salt, pepper, and cayenne pepper.

3. Reduce the heat, cover with a tight-fitting lid and simmer gently for 1½ hours. Add the zucchini and half of the parsley and cook for a further 15–20 minutes, stirring occasionally, until the meat is tender and the chickpeas are cooked. Stir in the remaining parsley and serve with bulgur wheat.

FOOD FACT

Bulgur or bulghur wheat, also known as cracked wheat and burghul, is a staple grain eaten throughout the Middle East. Already parboiled then dried and ground, bulgur is therefore quick to cook. It has a light texture and nutty taste. It is probably best known as the main ingredient of the Lebanese salad, tabbouleh, where it is combined with onions, parsley, and mint.

Serves 4–6 / Preparation time: 25 minutes, plus overnight soaking / Cooking time: 1¾ hours

North African Fish Stew with Couscous

1 cup dried chickpeas, soaked overnight,
    drained, and rinsed

2 onions, peeled

½ cup extra virgin olive oil

1–2 garlic cloves, sliced

1 celery stalk, sliced

1 red or green bell pepper, cored, seeded, and
    cut into strips

1 teaspoon Harissa (see page 20)

1 teaspoon ground cumin

3 cups ripe tomatoes, peeled
    and chopped

2 tablespoons tomato purée

2 carrots, sliced

large pinch of saffron threads

5 cups fish or chicken stock

1 pound instant couscous

2–2½ pounds firm white fish (such as bass,
    bream, snapper, cod), scaled, gutted, and cut
    into large pieces

3 tablespoons chopped parsley

3 tablespoons chopped cilantro

salt and pepper

1. Place the chickpeas in a saucepan and cover with water. Bring to a boil, reduce the heat, and simmer for about 1 hour, or until tender. Drain.

2. Cut the onions into wedges, keeping the root ends intact so that the layers do not separate. Heat the oil in a large flameproof casserole, add the onion wedges, garlic, and celery and cook for 10–12 minutes until softened and golden. Add the bell pepper, harissa, and ground cumin and cook for 5 minutes. Add the tomatoes, tomato purée, carrots, saffron, stock, and drained chickpeas. Bring to a boil, reduce the heat, and simmer gently for 15 minutes. Season to taste.

3. Meanwhile, cook the couscous according to the package instructions and keep warm.

4. Add the fish pieces to the stew and cook for 5 minutes, or until they are opaque. Stir in the herbs. Spoon the stew over the couscous to serve.

Serves 4 / Preparation time: 10 minutes / Cooking time: about 45 minutes

Rice and Lentil Pilaf

One-pot recipes like this one are a feature of the traditional cooking of Morocco, Algeria, and Tunisia, where it was more practical to use the minimum number of cooking pots.

¼ cup extra virgin olive oil

1 onion, finely chopped

4 garlic cloves, crushed

2 carrots, chopped

1 small eggplant, cubed

1 teaspoon ground ginger

1 teaspoon paprika

1 teaspoon ground coriander

1 teaspoon ground cumin

1 cup red lentils, rinsed

1 cup white long grain rice

4⅓ cups Vegetable Stock (see page 21)

4 cups spinach, washed and shredded

¼ cup sesame seeds, lightly toasted

salt and pepper

1. Heat the oil in a large heavy-based saucepan. Add the onion, garlic, carrots, and eggplant and fry for 5 minutes, stirring occasionally.

2. Stir the ginger, paprika, coriander, and cumin into the pan and cook, stirring, for 1 minute, then stir in the lentils and rice. When well mixed, add the stock. Bring to a boil, cover the pan, and simmer gently, stirring occasionally, for 30–35 minutes until the rice and lentils are tender and the stock has been absorbed.

3. Stir in the spinach and cook for 2 minutes until it has thoroughly wilted. Season to taste with salt and pepper and scatter with the sesame seeds.

Serves 4 / Preparation time: 10 minutes / Cooking time: 25 minutes

Ham Steaks
with Creamy Lentils

½ cup Puy lentils, rinsed

¼ cup butter

2 shallots

1 garlic clove, chopped

2 sprigs of thyme, crushed

1 teaspoon cumin seeds

4 teaspoons Dijon mustard

2 teaspoons clear honey

4 ham steaks

½ cup dry cider

⅓ cup light cream

salt and pepper

thyme leaves, to garnish

1. Place the lentils in a saucepan and cover with cold water. Bring to a boil and cook for 20 minutes.
2. Meanwhile, melt the butter in a frying pan and fry the shallots, garlic, thyme, and cumin seeds, stirring frequently, for 10 minutes, until the shallots are soft and golden.
3. Blend the mustard and honey together and season to taste with salt and pepper. Brush the mixture over the ham steaks and broil them for 3 minutes on each side, until golden and cooked through. Keep warm.
4. Drain the lentils and add them to the shallot mixture. Pour in the cider, bring to a boil, and cook until reduced to about ½ cup. Stir in the cream, heat through, and season to taste with salt and pepper. Serve the lentils with the ham steaks, garnished with thyme leaves.

Serves 4 / Preparation time: 20 minutes, plus overnight soaking / Cooking time: 1½ hours

Chicken Tagine with Rice and Chickpeas

1 cup dried chickpeas, soaked overnight, drained, and rinsed

½ cup lemon juice

pinch of crushed saffron threads

¼ cup extra virgin olive oil

4 chicken legs, thighs attached

2 large onions, chopped

2 large red bell peppers, cored, seeded, and thickly sliced lengthways

3 garlic cloves, crushed

1 red chili, seeded and finely chopped

1½ teaspoons ground cumin

1½ teaspoons ground coriander

stalks from a bunch of cilantro, chopped

1 ripe thin-skinned lemon, thinly sliced

¾ cup white long grain rice

2 cups chicken stock

1 cup mixed pitted green and black olives

salt and pepper

1. Cook the chickpeas in a saucepan of boiling water for 20 minutes. Drain.

2. Meanwhile, put the lemon juice into a small bowl, add the saffron threads, and leave to soak.

3. Heat the oil in a heavy-based flameproof casserole. Add the chicken legs and brown quickly. Remove from the casserole and place on paper towels to drain. Add the onions and red bell peppers to the pan and cook over a high heat, stirring frequently, until browned. Reduce the heat and stir in the garlic, chili, cumin, ground coriander, and cilantro stalks, lemon slices, rice, chickpeas, saffron liquid, and chicken stock. Return the chicken to the casserole, heat to simmering point, then cover and cook very gently for 30 minutes.

4. Scatter the olives over the casserole and push them into the liquid. Cover the casserole and cook for a further 30 minutes until the chicken is cooked and the chickpeas and rice are tender. Season to taste and serve hot.

Couscous, Chickpea, and Shrimp Salad

This easy-to-make salad offers an interesting combination of textures and flavors.

1½ cups cooked couscous

1 x 15-ounce can chickpeas, drained and rinsed

1 pound cooked and peeled shrimp

2 scallions, thinly sliced

3 well-flavored tomatoes, seeded and chopped

bunch of mint, chopped

lemon wedges, to serve

Dressing:

¾ cup extra virgin olive oil

⅓ cup lemon juice

pinch of superfine sugar

paprika

salt and pepper

1. To make the dressing, whisk together the oil and lemon juice in a small bowl or shake them together well in a screw-top jar. Add the sugar, paprika, and salt and pepper to taste.

2. Mix the couscous with the chickpeas, shrimp, scallions, tomatoes, and mint. Pour the dressing over the salad and toss well to coat all the ingredients. Serve with lemon wedges.

Serves 4–6 as an appetizer / Preparation time: 10 minutes

Fast Chickpea Salad

Canned chickpeas are a great product as they retain their flavor and texture and do away with the lengthy soaking and cooking time that dried ones require. This is a simple salad with the Mediterranean flavors of olive oil, garlic, lemon, and fresh parsley.

2 x 15-ounce cans chickpeas, drained
    and rinsed
6 scallions, finely sliced
1 red chili, seeded and finely sliced
½ cup chopped parsley
toasted pita or other warm bread, to serve

Dressing:
¾ cup extra virgin olive oil
1–2 garlic cloves, crushed
½ teaspoon finely grated lemon zest
⅓ cup lemon juice
salt and pepper

1. Place the chickpeas in a large serving bowl with the scallions, chili, and parsley.
2. Whisk together the dressing ingredients in a small bowl or place them in a screw-top jar and shake well to combine. Pour the dressing over the salad and toss to mix. Serve the salad with toasted pita or other warm bread.

Index

Acknowledgments

Executive Editor: Nicky Hill
Editor: Sharon Ashman
Senior Designer: Joanna Bennett
Production Controller: Jo Sim
Americanization: Dileri Johnston
Index: Indexing Specialists

Special Photography: William Reavell
Food Stylist: Oona van den Berg

All other photography Octopus Publishing Group
    Limited/David Loftus 52, 84, 99/Ian Wallace
    25, 136/Neil Mersh 55, 106/Peter Myers
    83/Roger Stowell 73/Sandra Lane 107,
    122/Sean Myers 29, 60, 114, 123,